Hello and welcome!

Dein *Wordmaster*-Heft hilft dir beim Wörterlernen.

In der Schule lernst du Englisch mit dem Buch *Go Ahead 5*.
Dort besprecht ihr auch die neuen Wörter einer Seite.

Danach machst du zuerst die Übung **New words** in deinem *Wordmaster*-Heft, die zu der neuen Seite in deinem Englischbuch gehört. Bei dieser Aufgabe fügst du die neuen Wörter in eine kleine Geschichte oder eine Unterhaltung ein und übst sie dadurch.

Wenn du mal nicht weiter weißt, darfst du im *Unit vocabulary* (Wörterverzeichnis) von *Go Ahead 5* (S.143–165) nachschauen.

Anschließend kannst du überprüfen, ob du alles richtig gelöst hast: Die Lösungen findest du im beigelegten Lösungsteil.

Wenn du sicher bist, dass die Lösung richtig ist, präge dir die Sätze ein. So behältst du die neuen Wörter besser!

Nach **New words** bietet der *Wordmaster* dann noch viele weitere Übungen zum Lernen der neuen Wörter, zum Beispiel Wortspiele und Rätsel.

Der *Wordmaster* gibt dir auch wichtige **Lerntipps** (auf Deutsch), die die Frage beantworten, wie man englische Wörter am besten lernt.

Am Ende jeder *Wordmaster*-Unit findest du dein **Learner log**, dein Lerntagebuch. Dort kannst du Fragen zu deinen Erfahrungen mit dem Wörterlernen beantworten.

Viel Spaß beim Englischlernen!

1 New words ▸ p. 6

Trage die englischen Begriffe für die deutschen Wörter in Klammern in die Lücken ein.

James **1** ________________ *(Mein Name ist)* Bond, James Bond.

Jessica **2** _________ *(Hallo)*, James.

James **3** _____________________________ *(Wie heißt du)*?

Jessica **4** _____ *(Ich bin)* Jessica. **5** I'm ________ *(aus)* Rosenheim.

6 I'm ____________ *(Deutsche)*. **7** ____________ *(Und Sie)*?

James **8** I ______ *(wohne)* in London. **9** I'm ____________ *(Engländer)*.

Jessica **10** ________________ *(Wie geht's Ihnen)*, James?

James **11** _____________ *(Mir geht's gut)*, ________________ *(danke)*.

12 What's _______ *(dein)* hobby, Jessica?

Jessica My hobby? James Bond films! **13** ______________ *(Auf Wiedersehen)*, James.

James **14** _____ *(Tschüss)*, Jessica.

2 Word search

Wörtersuche. In der Schlange sind zehn englische Wörter versteckt. Markiere sie.

Lerntipp

Wie merkst du dir die vielen englischen Wörter am besten? – Das musst du selbst herausfinden, denn jeder Mensch lernt anders. Probiere es mal mit diesen Vorschlägen:

Schreibe jedes Wort ab. • Sprich jedes Wort laut aus. • Schreibe jedes Wort im Zusammenhang.
• Zeichne so oft wie möglich etwas, das dir zu dem Wort einfällt – egal, was!

3 Jumbled sentences

Satzsalat. Bringe die Wörter dieser Sätze in die richtige Reihenfolge.
*(**Tipp:** Achte auf die Groß- und Kleinschreibung und die Satzzeichen.)*

1 Tim. I'm Hello. German. I'm — Hello. I'm Tim. I'm German.

2 is Hi. Lily. name My ____________________

3 London. I in I'm live Harry. ____________________

4 name? I'm your What's Mark. ____________________

5 Garmisch. Sophie. I'm I'm from ____________________

6 How Luke. you? Hello, are ____________________

7 you. And thank fine, you? I'm ____________________

4 Crossword puzzle

Kreuzworträtsel. Trage die Lösungen ein und du erhältst ein Lösungswort, das in die Sprechblase passt.

1 Deutsch; deutsch; Deutsche/r

2 gehen

3 von, aus

4 und

5 tschüss

6 mein, meine, mein

7 sehen

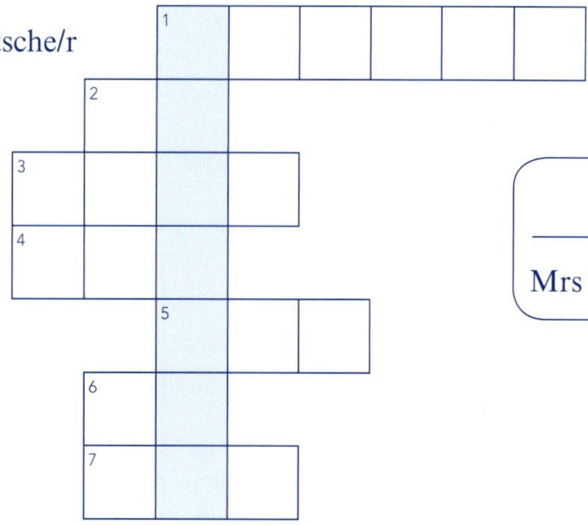

5 One word too many

Ein Wort zu viel. Finde das überflüssige Wort in jedem Satz und streiche es durch.

1 Hello. I'm Lana. I'm ~~from~~ English.

2 Hi. My name is I'm Alfie.

3 I'm Ruby. What's are your name?

4 I'm Jack. I no live in London.

5 How are you fine, Betty?

6 I'm is fine, thank you.

7 Bye, Sue. – My see you, Paul.

6 New words ▸ p. 7

Trage die englischen Begriffe für die deutschen Wörter in Klammern in die Lücken ein.

Hello. My name is Aysha. **1** I ♥ ______________ *(Farben)*. **2** I'm in my ________________ *(Klassenzimmer)* with Mrs Taylor, my ______________ *(Lehrerin)*. **3** ________________ *(Die Tafel)* in the classroom is __________ *(weiß)*. **4** __________________________ *(Welche Farbe hat)* the ________ *(Tür)*? **5** ______ *(Sie ist)* __________ *(grün)*. **6** My ________ *(Schreibtisch)* is ___________ *(gelb)* and my _________ *(Stuhl)* is _______ *(blau)*. **7** What's ______ *(rot)*? **8** _______________ *(Ein Apfel)*! **9** And what's in your ______ *(Tasche)*? **10** A green ______ *(Füller)*, a __________ *(schwarzer)* ___________ *(Bleistift)*, a white __________________________ *(Schulheft)* and a yellow ________ *(Buch)*. **11** Oh yes, and a red _________ *(Lineal)*! **12** And your _________________ *(Schirm)*? It's blue and green. **13** My _______________ *(Pullover)* and my _________ *(Hemd)* are blue, and Sarah's __________ *(Kleid)* is yellow and red. **14** Let's go ____ *(zu)* the _____________ *(Fenster)*. No, ________________________ *(es ist Zeit zu gehen)*. Bye!

7 The right colour

Die richtige Farbe. Lies die Sätze und male das Bild in den richtigen Farben aus. Wenn keine Farbe für den Gegenstand angegeben ist, male ihn nicht aus.

The door is yellow.
The board is white.
The desk is green.
The chair is red.

The bag is blue.
The book is black.
The shirt is red.
The sweater is blue.

The dress is yellow and green.
The apple is green.

8 Word partners

Bilde Wortpaare. Die Ballons helfen dir.

1 door – window

2 black – ______________________________

3 desk – ______________________________

4 pen – ______________________________

5 shirt – ______________________________

6 classroom – __________________________

9 The right word

Das richtige Wort. Unterstreiche das Wort, das in den Satz passt.

1 *I'm* / <u>*It's*</u> time to go.

2 *How* / *What* colour is your shirt?

3 It's the *door* / *dress* to my classroom.

4 Fatima's sweater *are* / *is* red and green.

5 The exercise book is in *you* / *your* bag.

6 The teacher is *from* / *in* the classroom.

7 What is it? – It's *a* / *an* umbrella.

8 Let's go *to* / *too* my classroom.

10 The missing letter

Der fehlende Buchstabe. Ergänze die fehlenden Buchstaben und finde das Lösungswort.

			1	A		P	L	E
2	Y	E	L	L		W		
		3	D	E		K		
				4		I	M	E
	5	R	U	L		R		
	6	B	O	A		D		

Lerntipp

- Bilde beim Lernen Gruppen von 6 bis 8 Wörtern.
- Schau dir die Wörter immer wieder an.
- Wiederhole regelmäßig – also oft!

11 New words ▸ p. 8

Trage die englischen Begriffe für die deutschen Wörter in Klammern in die Lücken ein.

1 ____________________ *(Hast du)* a dog? – **2** No, _____________ *(ich habe)* a _____ *(Katze)*.

3 Is ________ *(das dort)* your cat? – No, my cat is black.

4 I've got a ______ *(neues)* Taylor Swift poster. – **5** Oh. I've got a new ____________ *(Gitarre)*.

6 And _______ *(dies)* is my new bag. – OK. **7** And that is my ______ *(Bus)* – bye!

12 My book or your book?

Schreibe „This is" und „That's" in die richtige Sprechblase.

13 Jumbled sentences

Satzsalat. Bringe die Wörter dieser Sätze in die richtige Reihenfolge.

1 got you umbrella? a Have red ____________________________________

2 your guitar? colour new is What ____________________________________

3 new got a poster bag. and new I've a ____________________________________

14 What have you got?

Was besitzen diese Kinder? Male es in die Denkblasen.

"I've got a black cat."

"I've got a red guitar."

"I've got a green umbrella."

"I've got a new sweater."

15 New words ▸ p. 9

Trage die englischen Begriffe für die deutschen Wörter in Klammern in die Lücken ein.

Hello, Cathy. It's Maggie. **1** It's my ________________ *(Geburtstag)* today. … Thank you. **2** I'm ____________ *(elf)* _______ *(jetzt)*. **3** How ______ *(alt)* are you? Ten? **4** My brother is ten, ______ *(auch)*. **5** Can you come to my party __________ *(heute)*? Yes? **6** I'm ___________ *(glücklich)*! **7** Can you ____ *(sein)* ________ *(hier)* at four o'clock[1]?

16 Opposites

Gegensätze. Finde den passenden Gegensatz und trage ihn ein.

1 sit – stand

2 open – ______________________

3 Mrs – ______________________

4 thank you – ______________________

5 up – ______________________

6 go – ______________________

17 Classroom sentences

Was hat Herr Williams gerade gesagt? Lies die Beschreibung und schreibe den Satz.

1 (Ein Schüler steht neben Herrn Williams.) Come here, please.

2 (Ein Schüler steht an der Tafel.) ______________________

3 (Das Buch des Schülers ist geschlossen.) ______________________

4 (Das Buch des Schülers ist geöffnet.) ______________________

5 (Der Schüler sitzt.) ______________________

6 (Der Schüler steht.) ______________________

18 Word search

Im Suchrätsel befinden sich 9 englische Verben. Finde und markiere sie.

N	A	Y	S	I	T	O	P	D	I	C	N	G	U	L	M	Y	N	T	L	E	R
B	O	P	E	N	G	U	B	E	K	O	X	C	L	O	S	E	Y	W	I	L	G
P	R	U	D	C	O	R	T	Q	U	M	X	L	A	S	F	H	E	N	V	M	A
C	Y	S	T	A	N	D	G	R	U	E	M	A	Z	S	E	E	B	R	E	N	L

[1] **at four o'clock** um vier Uhr

19 New words ▸ pp. 10–12

Trage die englischen Begriffe für die deutschen Wörter in Klammern in die Lücken ein.

Hello. My name is Murat. I live in Hill Road. **1** My __________ number *(Hausnummer)* is 33. **2** I've got one ______________ *(Bruder)*, Kemal. **3** And I've got a __________ *(kleine)* ___________ *(Schwester)*, Layla. **4** ________________________ *(Ich habe keinen)* dog. **5** I've got eight ___ *(oder)* nine teddy __________ *(Teddybären)*! **6** ________________ *(Wie viele)* teddies have you got? **7** ____________'s *(Wo ist)* my new umbrella? **8** I can't ________ *(finden)* it. **9** 'Umbrella' is an English ________ *(Wort)*. **10** I can _________ *(buchstabieren)* it: U, M, B, R, E, L, L, A. Goodbye!

20 What's my name?

Lies die Aussagen, trage die Buchstaben an der richtigen Stelle ein, und du erhältst das Lösungswort.

Number five is an R. Number eleven is a K.

Number three is a C. Number eight is a J.

Number sixteen is an A. Number one is an A.

Number fourteen is an A. Number six is a P.

Number thirteen is an S. Number two is a C.

Number seventeen is an O. Number twelve is a W.

Number four is an N. Number fifteen is a T.

Number nine is an R. Number seven is a P.

Number ten is an I. Number eighteen is an A.

3	18	6	15	1	10	4

8	14	2	11

				R		
13	7	16	9	5	17	12

21 Odd word out

Ein Wort passt nicht. Finde und unterstreiche es.

1 red – blue – new – green

2 shirt – desk – dress – sweater

3 pen – pencil – ruler – number

4 you – I – it – or

5 old – open – sit – stand

6 what – where – white – how

7 teacher – poster – brother – sister

8 an – in – from – to

9 cat – dog – bear – song

10 five – four – fifteen – find

22 Questions and answers

Fragen und Antworten. Lies die Antworten und ergänze dann die Fragen dazu.

1 What's your name? – My name is Aysha.

2 ______ are you? – I'm fine, thanks.

3 ________ have you got? – I've got a new guitar.

4 And ____________ that? – That's a Rihanna poster.

5 ______ old are you, Aysha? – Eleven.

6 ________________ brothers and sisters have you got? – I've got two sisters.

7 ______________________ a brother, too? – No, I haven't got a brother.

8 __________ are your sisters now, Aysha? – My sisters are at school.

9 _____ you OK? – No, I'm not! Can I go now, please?

23 Picture puzzle

Bildrätsel. Welche Wörter stellen die Bilder dar? Trage sie ein und finde das Lösungswort.

24 The missing word

Das fehlende Wort. Ergänze die Sätze mit dem passenden Verb.

1 Can you __________ your name, please?
– It's K, Y, L, E.

2 I'm English. I __________ in London.

3 Where's my pen? – Let's __________ it.

4 __________ up, please.

5 Let's __________ happy today, OK?

6 Bye, Serena! – __________ you, Carlo!

7 __________ down, please.

8 Liz, it's 9.30. Time to __________!

9 __________ to the board, please.

25 The right word

Das richtige Wort. Ergänze die Sätze mit dem richtigen Wort (evtl. großgeschrieben) aus der Grafik.

1 Hi. My name is Andy. ________ from Berlin.

2 How are ________, Mr and Mrs Dalton?

3 The apple is in my bag. ________ green.

4 What's ________ name?

5 Have ________ got an umbrella, Mrs Lee?

6 ________ time to go.

7 I'm happy. ________ got a guitar. ________ new.

8 Is this ________ bag, Mr Miller?

9 That's Mrs Ling's bus. Can you see ________?

MY LEARNER LOG

Mein Lerntagebuch. Hier notierst du deine Erfahrungen mit dem Wörterlernen.

♥ Meine drei englischen Lieblingswörter aus dieser Unit sind:

____

☺ Ich finde, die drei einfachsten englischen Wörter in dieser Unit sind:

____

☹ Für mich sind die drei schwierigsten englischen Wörter in dieser Unit:

____

Englische Wörter zu lernen ist cool. ☐ anstrengend. ☐ lustig. ☐ einfach. ☐

1 New words ▸ p. 14

Trage die englischen Begriffe für die deutschen Wörter in Klammern in die Lücken ein.

Hello. My name is Leo. **1** ______________ *(Es gibt)* a ______________ *(Bild)* on my desk. **2** You can see my ____________ *(Familie)* in it. **3** The little _______ *(Mädchen)* is my sister Trudi. **4** ________________ *(Es gibt)* two _________ *(Hunde)*, too, Spot and Sandy. **5** I haven't got a ______________ *(Bild)* of my ____________ *(Freund)* Mykyta. **6** Mykyta is a ______ *(Junge)*, not a _______ *(Mädchen)*! **7** _____'s *(Er)* 11. Bye!

2 Crossword puzzle

Kreuzworträtsel. Trage die englischen Lösungen an der richtigen Stelle ein.

1						B	O	Y	
2						I			
3						R			
4						T			
5						H			
6						D			
7						A			
8						Y			

3 Jumbled sentences

Satzsalat. Bringe die Wörter dieser Sätze in die richtige Reihenfolge.

*(**Tipp:** Achte auf die Groß- und Kleinschreibung und die Satzzeichen.)*

1 the There's in family a picture. There's a family in the picture.

2 too. the are picture, dogs There in two ______________________________

3 and girls in four There boys house. are four the ______________________________

4 picture. He's the my There's in boy a friend. ______________________________

5 three There in are house. families the ______________________________

Lerntipp

Notiere dir neue Wörter als „Wortbilder" (s. Beispiel rechts).
Wie könnte ein „Wortbild" zu dem Wort *cat* aussehen?

4 New words ▸ p. 15

Trage die englischen Begriffe für die deutschen Wörter in Klammern in die Lücken ein.

Hi Elena,

1 I've got three pictures ______ *(für)* you today.

Picture one: **2** This is my family: ________ *(Mama)* and ______ *(Papa)* and __________ *(ihre)* brothers and sisters – I've got nine ________________ *(Tanten)* and ten _____________ *(Onkel)*! I've got two brothers, too. **3** ________ *(Sie)* are five and nine.

Picture two: This is Jake. **4** He's ____ *(auf)* Tim's birthday party. **5** ______ *(Seine)* __________________ *(feste Freundin)*, Emma, is in my __________ *(Klasse)*. **6** Mike, my ____________________ *(fester Freund)*, is a __________ *(Schüler)* at my ____________ *(Schule)*, too.

Picture three: This is Mr Ross. **7** He's the _____________________ *(Klassenlehrer)*.

8 He ___________ *(hat)* a new yellow sweater. **9** My school ________________ *(Schuluniform)* is red and blue. **10** OK, this is the ______ *(Ende)* for today.

Bye,

Melinda

5 People

Menschen. Sortiere die Wörter für Menschen in die richtige Liste ein.

~~auntie~~ • boy • boyfriend • brother • dad • friend • German • girl • girlfriend • Mr • Mrs • mum • pupil • sister • teacher • tutor • uncle

1 Wörter **nur** für Mädchen/Frauen:

auntie, ____

2 Wörter **nur** für Jungen/Männer:

____

3 Wörter für Mädchen/Frauen **und** Jungen/Männer: ____

6 Missing words

Fehlende Wörter. Ergänze den Text mit den richtigen Wörtern.

Omar ______ **(1)** got a new friend. ______ **(2)** name ___ **(3)** Thomas. Omar and Thomas ______ **(4)** pupils at Hillside School. ________ **(5)** are in Class 7PS. PS is for Philip Shaw, __________ **(6)** class tutor.

7 New words ▸ p. 16

Trage die englischen Begriffe für die deutschen Wörter in Klammern in die Lücken ein.

Lizzy **1** This is a ________ *(sehr)* ________ *(gutes)* book. **2** There's a __________ *(großartig)* ________________ *(Foto von)* a dog on _________ *(Seite)* 14. Have you got a dog?

Emma **3** No, ____ *(wir)* haven't got a dog. Can we go now, please?

Lizzy **4** The book has got a good __________________________ *(Einführung)*, too.

5 ______ *(Aber)* the ___________________ *(Übungen)* are ___________ *(schrecklich)*!

Emma Oh, they're OK. Let's go now, Lizzy. **6** It's ________ *(spät)*.

Lizzy Yes, yes. We've got time. **7** The school is five _______________ *(Minuten)* from here. Our new teacher, Mrs Harris, isn't English. **8** _______'s *(Sie)* __________________ *(Amerikanerin)*.

Emma **9** Yes, Mrs Harris is very ________ *(nett)*, but …

Lizzy **10** Mrs Harris' ____________________ colour *(Lieblingsfarbe)* is blue. And she …

Emma (**11** This is an awful ___________________ *(Situation)*. What can I do? **12** I can go to school ________ *(mit)* Anna!) **13** ________________ *(Tut mir leid)*, Lizzy. Bye!

8 'sie / Sie'

Finde und ergänze das richtige englische Wort für das deutsche 'sie / Sie'.

1 Are ________ Mrs Black?

2 Bella is my sister. ________ isn't very nice.

3 This is my school uniform. ________ isn't new.

4 The pupils at my new school are OK. ________ aren't awful.

9 Colour the words

Markiere die Wörter im Kasten. Personen: blau; Dinge: rot; Tätigkeiten: grün; Eigenschaften: gelb.

old	picture	awful	sit	pupil	see	desk	fine
new	spell	uniform	tutor	bag	open	uncle	star

10 Missing words

Fehlende Wörter. Ergänze die Sätze mit den richtigen Wörtern. Sie sind alle in der Wortschlange enthalten.

1 Hi, I'm Dan. I'm here _______ my dog, Sandy.

2 I'm not German. I'm _______ England.

3 I live _______ London.

4 I'm _______ Elton School.

5 I've got new photos _______ my favourite football stars.

6 The German word _______ 'football' is 'Fußball'.

7 Sorry, it's time _______ go now.

11 Crossword puzzle

Kreuzworträtsel. Wie heißen die deutschen Wörter im Kasten auf Englisch? Setze die Antworten der Reihe nach von oben nach unten geschrieben ein.

~~sechs~~
finden
großartig
tut mir leid
Foto
gut
schrecklich
nett, schön, hübsch
spät
sein/e
von
Ende

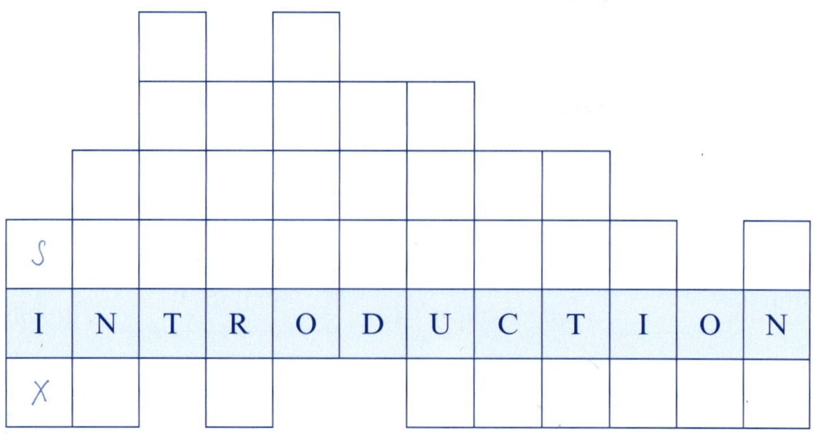

12 One word too many

Ein Wort zu viel. Finde das überflüssige Wort in jedem Satz und streiche es durch.

1 Nicki Minaj is nice, but she isn't for my favourite star.

2 I've got with ten great photos of my favourite star, Lana Del Rey.

3 Jack, we're of ten minutes late for the film!

13 New words ▸ p. 17

Trage die englischen Begriffe für die deutschen Wörter in Klammern in die Lücken ein.

1 We've got six lessons *(Unterrichtsstunden)* today. **2** The firs *(erste)* lesson *(Unterrichtsstunde)* is math *(Mathematik)*. **3** Mrs Scott, the teacher, has got a French *(französischen)* boyfriend. **4** I'm sure *(sicher)* he's nice. **5** I've got a good poster in my room *(Zimmer)*. It's a picture of Paris. Paris is great! Where's Mrs Scott now? **6** She's there *(dort)*, at the door. **7** A group *(Gruppe)* of pupils is with her. **8** There's a school party at the end of this week *(Woche)* with great mousic *(Musik)*. **9** It's the first *(erste)* party this year *(Jahr)*.

14 Jumbled partner words

Wortsalat. Bringe die Buchstaben der Wortpaare in die richtige Reihenfolge.

1 etvlew twelve – nigehete eighteen
2 necFhr French – nreamG German
3 sheuo house – omor room
4 yddeWensa Wednesday – hauyrdTs Thursday
5 cohosl school – nosesl lessor
6 kewe week – arey year

15 Questions and answers

Fragen und Antworten. Welche Antwort passt zu welcher Frage? Ziehe Linien.

1 Am I late?	**a)** Yes, I am.
2 Is Anna nice?	**b)** No, it isn't.
3 Are you sure?	**c)** Yes, we are.
4 Is this my chair?	**d)** Yes, they are.
5 Is Sven French?	**e)** No, you aren't.
6 Are Liz and Sue in your group?	**f)** Yes, she is.
7 Are we friends?	**g)** No, he isn't.

16 New words ▸ pp. 18–19

Trage die englischen Begriffe für die deutschen Wörter in Klammern in die Lücken ein.

1 ____________________ *(Du bist gut dran)*, Marc. **2** You haven't got a sister, __________ *(richtig)*? **3** My sister June is a ________ *(albern)* girl. **4** I ____________________ *(manchmal)* go shopping with ______ *(ihr)*. It's awful. But shopping with Uncle Lou is great! **5** He's my ______________________________ *(Lieblingsperson)* in the family. Here he is. **6** Are you __________ *(bereit)*, Uncle Lou? Let's go!

17 Some words rhyme

Manche Wörter reimen sich. Schau dir die Bälle an und suche für jedes Wort das richtige Reimwort aus.

1 year – here

2 there – ____________

3 end – ____________

4 her – ____________

5 late – ____________

6 he – ____________

7 too – ____________

8 white – ____________

18 The right word

Das richtige Wort. Unterstreiche das Wort, das in den Satz passt.

1 My little brother can be a very *silly / sure* boy sometimes.

2 You're *late / lucky*. You haven't got a brother.

3 Shopping? Yes, please! I'm *ready / sorry*.

4 Mrs Green is a good teacher. – You're *great / right*.

5 This is Jenny. *Her / Their* brother's name is Johnny.

19 Word search

Im Suchrätsel befinden sich 12 englische Wörter, die mit S anfangen. Finde und markiere sie.

B	A	S	P	E	L	L	S	U	S	S	I	T	U	A	T	I	O	N	I	N	S
O	S	Y	N	S	O	M	E	T	I	M	E	S	S	H	I	R	T	R	S	O	O
S	P	T	S	I	K	S	I	M	T	A	S	H	O	L	S	I	L	L	Y	S	N
D	O	S	U	R	E	Z	S	Y	L	S	E	E	B	S	C	H	O	O	L	D	G

20 New words ▸ p. 21

Trage die englischen Begriffe für die deutschen Wörter in Klammern in die Lücken ein.

Jack **1** Dad, can we go to Auntie Sarah's ______________________ *(am Wochenende)*?

Dad OK, Jack. **2** We can go __________________ *(am Samstag)* ____ *(um)*

ten ______ *(nach)* three.

Jill **3** But Dad, it's ____________ *(Fußball)* on Saturday!

4 It's ___ *(um)* ____________________ *(halb drei)*.

Dad OK, Jill. **5** Let's go to Auntie Sarah's at ____________ *(Viertel)* to five.

Jen **6** But Dad, please, it's Dave's party ___ *(um)* six ___________ *(Uhr)*!

Dad **7** OK, OK, Jack, Jill and Jen. Saturday isn't the right _____ *(Tag)*.

Let's go to Auntie Sarah's on Sunday.

21 The right word

Welches Wort gehört in die Lücke? Trage es ein.

1 School is ________ 7.30 ________ 12.45.

2 There's no school ________ the weekend.

3 Football is ________ Wednesday.

4 ______ twelve o'clock it's maths.

22 The right time

Trage die Zeiten (als Ziffern) und ein Stichwort in Ritas Kalender ein und markiere ihren freien Tag.

1 Joe's birthday party is from six o'clock to half past eight on Saturday.

2 It's football from quarter to six to half past seven on Friday.

3 My bus to London is at twenty-five to five on Tuesday.

4 My friend Paolo comes at quarter past four on Thursday.

5 The new film is from quarter past six to twenty to eight on Wednesday.

6 My guitar lesson is from half past two to quarter past three on Monday.

Monday	Tuesday	Wednesday	Thursday	Friday	Saturday	Sunday
					6.00 – 8.30: Joe's party	

23 New words ▸ p. 22

Trage die englischen Begriffe für die deutschen Wörter in Klammern in die Lücken ein.

Sam We're late! **1** Let's ________ *(verlassen)* the shop now.

Mum We aren't late. **2** We're ____________ *(pünktlich)*.

Sam No, Mum. **3** Can you _________ *(dich beeilen)*, please?

Mum OK, OK. **4** What's on _________________ *(Fernsehen)* today?

Sam **5** It's the Hip Hop Music Show at six o'clock. I ______ *(mag)* hip hop.

Mum **6** Sure, but it's ______________ *(die gleiche)* music _________ *(jeden)* ______________ *(Morgen)*, __________________ *(Nachmittag)* and _____________ *(Abend)*.

7 And you watch TV in ______ *(Bett)*. That's awful.

Sam **8** And you always ________ *(liest)* im Bett. That's awful, too!

Mum OK, OK. **9** First you can watch TV. ________ *(Dann)* we can play a game. OK?

Sam OK. **10** But can we go _________ *(aus … hinaus)* the shop NOW?!

A At home *(Zuhause)*

1 home
(Heim, Zuhause)

2 get up
(aufstehen)

3 make homework
(Hausaufgaben machen)

4 watch TV
(fernsehen) [Kurzform]

5 play computer games
(Computerspiele spielen)

B On the road *(Unterwegs)*

1 away
(weg, fort)

2 steet
(Straße)

3 way
(Weg)

4 drive
(fahren)

5 car
(Auto)

6 mile
(Meile)

7 near
(nah)

24 Picture puzzle

Bilderrätsel. Schau dir die Zeichnung an und finde sieben weitere Dinge.

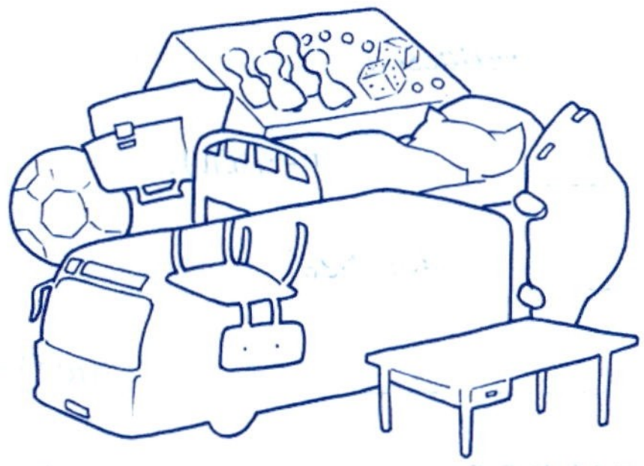

game
table
football
bus

bed
car
chair
bag

25 English–German crossword

Englisch–deutsches Kreuzworträtsel. Trage die deutsche Bedeutung der englischen Wörter ein.

Across ▸

1 morning
6 (to) read
7 work
10 (to) get up
12 on time

Down ▾

1 mile
2 (to) play
3 (to) leave
4 away
5 car
8 then
9 way
11 near

26 Jumbled sentences and words

Satz- und Wortsalat. Bringe die Wörter dieser Sätze in die richtige Reihenfolge.
Achtung: In jedem Satz sind auch die mittleren Buchstaben eines Wortes durcheinander geraten.

1 ~~ten~~ ~~It's~~ in to school car. the *mitunes* It's ten ______

2 three The in home *afonerton.* go at half pupils past the ______

3 I the sometimes in *teiesvlion* evening. watch ______

4 my out weekend At *gierrflind.* the I with go ______

27 New words ▸ p. 23

Trage die englischen Begriffe für die deutschen Wörter in Klammern in die Lücken ein.

Come to FreeFun Holiday Camp! It's a great camp for kids near London. **1** You can't speak *(sprechen)* English? **2** Now *(Nun)*, you can learn *(lernen)* it at the camp. **3** You can listen *(zuhören)* music, too – or sing *(singen)* with the group. **4** You can't play the piano *(Klavier)* or the guitar? **5** learn *(Lerne)* it here. **6** Can you swim *(schwimmen)*? No? **7** Of course *(Natürlich)* you can learn *(lernen)* it here! **8** Fly *(Fliege)* to London and come to FreeFun Holiday Camp!

28 Too many verbs

Zu viele Verben. Wähle für jeden Satz das passende Verb aus dem Kasten. Achte auch auf die richtige Form des Verbs!

1 Let's sing a song.
2 I can speak French.
3 Mum watches TV in the evening.
4 Rusty can swim.
5 Let's fly to New York.
6 Mel does her homework in her room.
7 Sh! Let's listen to the song.
8 I can't play the piano.

29 Odd word out

Ein Wort passt nicht. Finde und unterstreiche es.

1 morning – day – afternoon – evening
2 like – listen – speak – see
3 song – guitar – bag – piano
4 be – get up – hurry – leave
5 happy – awful – great – nice
6 fly – swim – drive – sit
7 game – music – work – television
8 learn – play – read – spell

Lerntipp
Lernt zu zweit! Zum Beispiel liest eine/r die deutschen (oder die englischen) Wörter aus dem Wörterverzeichnis im Buch vor und der/die andere „übersetzt" sie.

30 New words ▸ p. 24

Trage die englischen Begriffe für die deutschen Wörter in Klammern in die Lücken ein.

Where are you, Joey? **1** Oh, you're on (*auf*) my bed. **2** You're very quiet (*ruhig*) today, Joey. What? **3** Well, I can't always (*immer*) be here in the room with you. **4** Sometimes I go to the bathroom (*Badezimmer*). **5** And sometimes I'm in the kitchen (*Küche*). What? **6** Yes, there's a sandwich (*belegtes Brot*) on the table (*Tisch*) here. No, you can't have it! – Joey, what time is it? **7** I haven't got my watch (*Armbanduhr*). Let's hurry, Joey. I'm sure it's late. Let's get into the car. **8** You think (*denkst*) you can drive the car today? **9** No, Joey, it's my turn (*ich bin an der Reihe*). What? **10** Who is (*Wer ist*) Honey? Your girlfriend?? No, she can't come with us. Let's go now.

31 Questions

Fragen. Ergänze jede Frage mit dem passenden Fragewort.

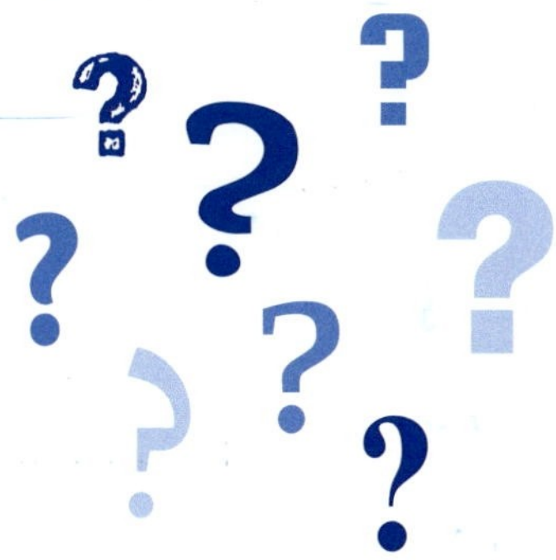

1 Who 's in the bathroom? – It's Sophie.

2 How are you today, Sophie? – I'm fine, thanks.

3 What 's the problem, Adam? – I can't get in the bathroom.

4 What time is it? – It's twenty-five past eight.

5 Where 's your watch, Sophie? – I think it's in my room.

32 The little words

Ergänze jeden Satz mit dem passenden „kleinen" Wort. Die Schilder helfen dir.

1 In the morning Luke gets ~~out~~. up

2 He listens to the radio in the bathroom.

3 Then he sits ~~in~~ in the kitchen. down

4 The cornflakes are on the table.

5 Hurry up, Luke! It's late.

6 Let's go ~~down~~ of the house now. out

7 Great, Luke. Now get in the car.

33 New words pp. 25–29

Trage die englischen Begriffe für die deutschen Wörter in Klammern in die Lücken ein.

Hi, I'm Henry. I can play the piano. **1** I ~~team~~ practise *(übe)* every day. My sister can't play the piano. **2** She's very silly for her age *(Alter)*. **3** We aren't a very good team *(Team)*. **4** She sometimes goes to the disco *(Disco)* on Saturdays. I can't go. **5** I've got double *(doppelte)* piano lessons in my timetable *(Stundenplan)* for Saturday evenings.

34 Word groups

Ergänze jede Wortgruppe mit dem passenden Wort.

1 years – old – a g e

2 school – lessons – t i m e t a b l e

3 music – pop – d i s c o

4 class – group – t e a m

5 computer – television – t e l e p h o n e

6 think – learn – p r a c t i s e

35 Two words

Ergänze jeden Satz mit zwei passenden Wörtern aus dem Kasten.

~~age~~ • ~~always~~ • ~~bag~~ • ~~happy~~ • ~~house~~ • ~~practise~~ • ~~problem~~ • ~~quiet~~ • ~~sometimes~~ • ~~speak~~ • ~~telephone~~ • ~~watch~~

1 What's your *problem* / *age*?

2 What's your house / telephone number? ✓

3 Julie and Jim are very quiet / sometimes.

4 Let's practise / speak German at the weekend. ✓

5 I always / happy get up late on Sundays.

6 I can't find my bag / watch. ✓

36 Some words rhyme

Welche Wortpaare reimen sich (✔) und welche nicht (✘)?

1 lead – read ✔

2 time – team ✘

3 way – fly ✘

4 who – you ✓

5 long – song ✓

6 quiet – right ✘

7 road – good ✘

8 age – page ✓

37 Kevin's day

a) *Unterstreiche das Wort, das in den Satz passt.*

1 Jessy comes to my *bed* / *desk* at seven o'clock every morning.

2 I get *in* / *up* at ten past seven and go out with her.

3 Then she's in the *bathroom* / *kitchen* with me. She likes cornflakes!

4 Sometimes we play a little game: *Where's* / *Who's* my sandwich? Jessy always finds it.

5 Jessy can't come to school, but I always hurry *home* / *house* in the afternoon.

6 Then we go out for a *good* / *long* time. That's great.

7 In the evening Jessy *sees* / *watches* TV and I do my homework.

8 And then it's time for bed. I go to my bed and she goes on her *car* / *chair*.

See you in the morning, Jessy!

b) *Who's Jessy? Tick ✔ the right answer.*

Kevin's girlfriend. ☐ Kevin's dog. ☐ Kevin's little sister. ☐

38 What is it?

Was ist gemeint? Die Buchstaben in der falschen Reihenfolge rechts helfen dir.

1 I can't play it. ____________________ naipo

2 I sometimes listen to it. ____________________ ordai

3 I play games on it. ____________________ trumpeco

4 My mum drives to work in it. ____________________ rac

5 I sometimes watch it in the evening. ____________________ vistelione

6 I do it in the afternoon. ____________________ whomroke

Lerntipp

Manchen Kindern hilft es, wenn sie sich neue Wörter musikalisch merken.
Versuche doch einmal, die Wörter zu singen. Du kannst auch ein kleines Lied daraus machen.
Es muss sich nicht reimen.

Beispiel Auf die Melodie von „Fuchs, du hast die Gans gestohlen" kann man singen:

I have got a sister,
Brother, mum and dad.
Brother, mum and dad.
My sister's name is Anna/…,
My brother's name is Max/….

39 Boxes

Was befindet sich in den Kisten? Gib jeder Kiste eine passende Überschrift.

1 question words
2 number words
3 coulure words
4 week days
5 fumily parts
6 school lessons
7 in the house
8 in the school bag

MY LEARNER LOG

Mein Lerntagebuch. Hier notierst du deine Erfahrungen mit dem Wörterlernen.

♥ Meine drei englischen Lieblingswörter aus dieser Unit sind:

____

Ich kann jetzt auf Englisch …

– die Uhrzeit sagen *(Schau auf deine Uhr. Wie spät ist es?)*: ______________________________

____

– über meine Familie sprechen *(Nenne deine Familienmitglieder.)*: ______________________________

____

– über meinen Alltag sprechen *(Beschreibe kurz den Tagesablauf bei euch zu Hause.)*: ______________________________

____

____

Wie gut hat das geklappt? Ich gebe mir folgende Schulnoten (von 1–6):

– die Uhrzeit sagen: *Note:* ☐

– über meine Familie sprechen: *Note:* ☐

– über meinen Alltag sprechen: *Note:* ☐

1 New words ▸ p. 30

Trage die englischen Begriffe für die deutschen Wörter in Klammern in die Lücken ein.

This is my house. **1** We're in the ~~floor~~ hall *(Flur)*, on the ground floor *(Erdgeschoss)*. ✗
This is the kitchen. **2** It's very small *(klein)*. **3** There's a table in the eating room *(Esszimmer)*. **4** This is the living room *(Wohnzimmer)*. We always watch TV here.
5 My bedroom is on the first floor *(ersten Stock)*. **6** What about *(Wie ist es mit)* you? **7** Have you got your own *(eigenes)* sleeping room *(Schlafzimmer)*, too?
8 There's a garage *(Garage)* ~~back~~ behind *(hinter)* the house. **9** Oh yes, and there's a ✗
garden *(Garten)* ~~for~~ infront of *(vor)* the house. My sister isn't here. **10** She has ✗
got a flat *(Wohnung)* in London now.

Lerntipp
Oft lassen sich Wörter besser behalten, wenn man sie in einem Wortnetz darstellt:

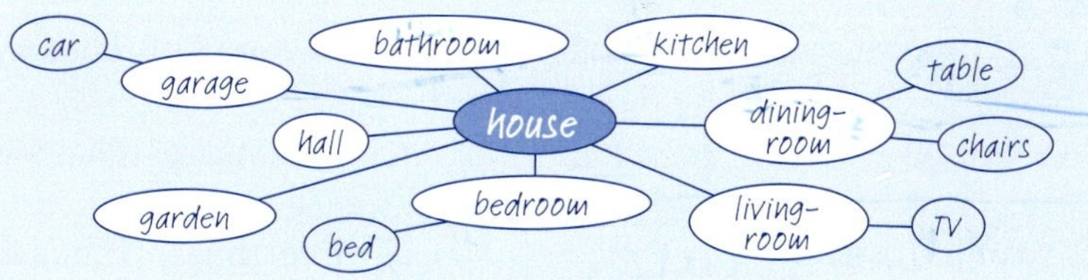

2 Puzzle

Ergänze die Sätze und trage die markierten Buchstaben an der richtigen Stelle unten ein.

1 The Taylors haven't got a house. They've got a f l a t.
2 Let's open the Taylors' door. Where are we? We're in the h a l l.
3 There's a sofa and a TV in the Taylors' l i v i n g - r o o m.
4 The Taylors have got two ~~bed~~ ~~b a t h r o o m~~, one for mum and dad and one for Luke and Ray. bedrooms
5 There's a table and six chairs in the d i n i n g - r o o m
6 The Taylors haven't got their own g a r a g e …

… but they've got a G ~~A~~ R A G O for their car.
5 1 3 2 6 4

3 Jumbled sentences

Satzsalat. Bringe die Wörter dieser Sätze in die richtige Reihenfolge.

1 ~~you~~ front house? the ~~Can~~ car in see the of Can you see the car in front of the house
2 her Alice own got bedroom. has Alice has got her own bedroom
3 a the garden There's house. small behind There's a small garden behind the house.

4 New words ▸ p. 31

Trage die englischen Begriffe für die deutschen Wörter in Klammern in die Lücken ein.

Hello Liang, I can make a film of my house and garden for you. **1** There's a little camera *(Kamera)* in my mobile phone[1]. **2** Let's go out of *(um … herum)* the house. **3** Can you see that Mountain *(Berg)*? It's the Högl. What's that? **4** It's Pia's recket *(Tennisschläger)*. Pia is my sister. **5** I've got my own racket *(Tennisschläger)*. **6** It's in my wardroh *(Kleiderschrank)*. And there's Pia. Can you see her? **7** She's in front of the stereo *(Stereogerät)* in the living-room. Bye for today, Jonas

5 Funny words

Komische Wörter. Ersetze den falschen Teil des Wortes mit dem richtigen.

1. Sometain? That's wrong! It's sometimes.
2. Wardrite? That's wrong! It's wardrobe.
3. Piction? That's wrong! It's picture.
4. Televicise? That's wrong! It's television.
5. Favourobe? That's wrong! It's favourite.
6. Mounture? That's wrong! It's mountain.
7. Exertimes? That's wrong! It's exercise.
8. Situasion? That's wrong! It's situation.

6 What is it?

Was ist gemeint? Gib eine Antwort. Die Bilder rechts helfen dir.

1. You play tennis with it. – It's a tennis racket
2. It's where your shirts, sweaters and dresses are. – It's a weardrob.
3. My mobile phone has got one (for photos). – It's a kamera.
4. It's the car's "bedroom". – It's a garage.
5. You listen to music with it. – It's a radio.

7 Questions

Fragen. Ergänze die Fragen mit Do oder Have.

1. Do you like music? – Well, I like pop music.
2. Have you got a piano? – No, but I've got a guitar.
3. Do you play tennis? – No, but I play football.
4. Have you got a camera? – Well, there's a camera in my mobile phone.

[1] **mobile phone** [məʊbaɪl 'fəʊn] Mobiltelefon, Handy

8 New words ▸ p. 32

Trage die englischen Begriffe für die deutschen Wörter in Klammern in die Lücken ein.

Who am I? **1** That's a very silly ____________ *(Frage)*!

2 The ____________ *(Antwort)* is: I'm Tina, Tina Fox, of course.

3 I like ____________ *(Sport)*. Do you like sport, too? I play football.

4 ____________ *(Kennst)* du Arsenal? They're great!

5 We can ____________ *(tauschen)* football pictures. What do you think?

6 Oh, my ____________ *(Mutter)* ____________ *(sagt)*, "Be ____________ *(still)*, Tina."

7 My brother always ____________ *(macht)* his homework in the evening. See you tomorrow. Bye!

9 Questions and answers

Welche Antwort passt zu welcher Frage? Ziehe Linien.

1 Have you got a tennis racket?
2 Do you know Hassan's mother?
3 Can we swap football pictures?
4 Has Amy got a camera?
5 Does your boyfriend like sport?
6 Can I leave now?

a) Yes, of course. Bye.
b) No, but she has got a mobile phone.
c) No, I don't know her.
d) No, I don't play tennis.
e) Yes, we can. Great!
f) Yes, he likes football.

10 Odd word out

Ein Wort passt nicht. Finde und unterstreiche es.

1 desk – answer – bed – wardrobe
2 maths – music – question – sport
3 bedroom – kitchen – racket – hall
4 mother – mini-golf – tennis – football
5 stereo – flat – camera – telephone
6 say – sing – speak – small

11 Word search

Im Suchrätsel befinden sich 12 englische Verben. Finde und markiere sie.

B	R	A	V	S	K	N	O	W	L	A	T	L	I	K	E	L	S	W	I	M	T	F
A	C	R	E	A	D	G	R	O	N	L	E	A	R	N	Y	W	A	T	C	H	A	L
E	T	H	I	N	K	B	U	L	E	S	W	A	P	P	L	A	Y	H	U	R	R	Y
T	R	O	U	D	R	I	V	E	P	E	L	S	C	H	O	N	G	R	A	M	S	E

12 New words ▸ p. 33

Trage die englischen Begriffe für die deutschen Wörter in Klammern in die Lücken ein.

Jack 1 Can I go to the park *(Park)* on your bike *(Fahrrad)*?

Sue 2 You can't drive *(fahren)* my bike *(Fahrrad)*. You're too small.

Jack 3 OK. Can I walk *(laufen)* to the supermarket *(Supermarkt)*?

Sue No, you can't. You're too small. Hm, do you know what?

4 We can make your father *(Vater)* happy.

5 Let's work *(arbeiten)* in the garden.

13 Synonyms and opposites

a) *Synonyme. Wähle Wörter aus dem Kasten, die die gleiche oder eine ähnliche Bedeutung haben, und trage sie ein.*

~~father~~ • ~~great~~ • happy • ~~leave~~ • ~~little~~ • ~~mum~~ • new • sister • teacher • work

1 mother – mum

2 father – dad

3 very nice – great

4 little – small

5 go away – leave

b) *Gegensätze. Wähle Wörter aus dem Kasten, die die entgegengesetzte Bedeutung haben, und trage sie ein.*

always • ~~answer~~ • ~~awful~~ • know • ~~no~~ • now • ~~old~~ • ~~open~~ • sure • swap

1 yes – no

2 old – new

3 great – awful

4 open – close

5 question – answer

14 Verbs

Verben der Fortbewegung. Trage die englischen Wörter/Ausdrücke ein.

1 *(zu Fuß)* ____________

2 *(mit zwei Rädern)* ________ a ________

3 *(mit vier Rädern)* ________ a ________

4 *(im Wasser)* ____________

5 *(in der Luft)* ____________

15 New words ▸ p. 34

Trage die englischen Begriffe für die deutschen Wörter in Klammern in die Lücken ein.

Harry Do you know Ally Lee? **1** She's ______________ *(wundervoll)*! Ally's father plays football for Arsenal.

Yusuf **2** No, that's ________ *(falsch)*. **3** Ally's father works at a ______________________ *(Tankstelle)*.

Harry Oh, OK. **4** But Ally's mother has got a _____ *(Arbeitsplatz)* at a ________ *(Bank)*.

Yusuf That isn't right. **5** Ally's mother works for a computer ______________ *(Computerfirma)*.

Harry **6** ___ *(Äh)*, and Ally ______________ *(unterstützt)* Manchester United.

Yusuf No, she likes Arsenal.

Harry **7** And Ally's ______________ *(Eltern)* drive ______________________ *(Formel 1-)* cars.

Yusuf No, they don't. They haven't got a car.

Harry No? **8** Well, your father is a ______________ *(Postbote)* and always ________________ *(kommt nach Hause)* at four.

Yusuf That's right!

16 Work

Markiere jedes Wort: Nimm blau für Berufsbezeichnungen und rot für Arbeitsstätten.

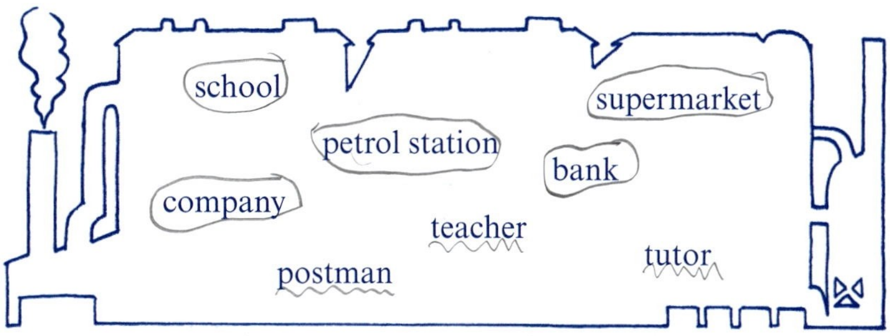

17 The right word

Das richtige Wort. Unterstreiche das Wort, das in den Satz passt.

1 My mother has got a new *work* / *job* at a bank.

2 She gets *house* / *home* late in the evening.

3 My parents are very happy. They've got *a fantastic* / *an awful* new car.

4 They always *drive* / *ride* the car to the same petrol station.

5 My friend's father *leaves* / *works* at that petrol station.

6 He *supports* / *swaps* Manchester United.

18 New words ▸ pp. 38–39

Trage die englischen Begriffe für die deutschen Wörter in Klammern in die Lücken ein.

1 My sisters play basketball *(Basketball)*. **2** I sometimes play with them *(ihnen)*. Their boyfriends play football. **3** But they don't play with us *(uns)*. **4** look *(Schau)*! That's Marcella. **5** Can you see she *(sie)*? She's with her boyfriend. **6** I don't like him *(ihn)* – and he doesn't like me *(mich)*.

19 Pronouns

Pronomen. Ergänze die Sätze mit dem richtigen Wort.
Wenn du Hilfe brauchst, schau dir die Tasche rechts genauer an.

1 Where are Fatima and Joe? I can't see them.

2 Eva is my friend. I go to school with her.

3 Is that your new bag? I like it.

4 Who's that boy? I think I know him.

5 I've got two brothers. Look, this is a picture of him.

6 I'm here! Can you see me?

20 The right word

Das richtige Wort. Unterstreiche das Wort, das in den Satz passt.

1 Where's my watch? I can't find *her* / *him* / *it*.

2 Lara is my girlfriend. *He* / *Her* / *She* is fantastic.

3 There's Mum. I think she can't see *her* / *them* / *us*. Mum, here we are!

4 Let's go now, Sam. *They* / *Us* / *We* are late.

5 The new pupils are nice. I like *him* / *them* / *they*.

6 Where's my book? Oh no! Tim and Tom, *we* / *you* / *your* are awful!

Lerntipp

Gerade Pronomen lassen sich besser behalten, wenn du sie als Sätze über deine Familie, deine Freundinnen und Freunde oder Lehrer/innen aufschreibst, z.B.:

Mrs Meier is my English teacher. She's nice. I like her.
Jörn is my cousin. He's fourteen. I've got a photo of him.

26 Two words
1 bank / petrol station
2 behind / in front of
3 hall / living-room
4 fantastic / wrong
5 round / up
6 bad / small

27 Odd word out
1 racket 2 question 3 plan
4 camera 5 bank 6 park
7 answer 8 swap

28 A funny poem
6 – 2 – 7 – 1 – 4 – 8 – 5 – 3

Unit 3

1 New words
1 pet, hamster
2 called
3 wheel, cage
4 rabbits
5 hutches
6 run, around
7 rabbits, eat, grass, feeds
8 lets, out, lunch-time

2 The right verb
2 open
3 go
4 find
5 feed

3 New words
1 mice 2 farmer 3 gun 4 mice
5 mouse 6 budgies 7 smell 8 stew

4 Funny pets
2a + 1b = rabbit
3a + 4b = budgie
4a + 5b = dog
5a + 2b = mouse
6a + 3b = cat

5 Jumbled sentences
1 My friend's cat is called Tiddles.
2 Hamsters like a wheel in their cage.
3 Can I feed your dog today?
4 Don't let the mice out!
5 The budgie's cage doesn't smell very good.
6 Rabbits live in hutches and they like grass.

6 New words
1 our
2 neighbours
3 give, its
4 tea
5 those
6 shoes
7 These, shoes
8 then

7 Missing letters
2 budgie
3 cage
4 eat
5 feed
6 hutch
7 lunch
8 neighbour
9 pet
10 rabbit
11 shoe
12 wheel

8 Right or wrong?
2 ✘
3 ✔
4 ✔
5 ✔
6 ✘

9 The right word
1 its, It's
2 They're, Their
3 you're, your

10 New words
1 people, bus-stop
2 men
3 man, children
4 women
5 woman, baby
6 child

11 Plurals
1 baby, Baby, Babys
2 bus-stop, bus-stops, Bushaltestellen
3 cages, Käfig, Käfige
4 budgie, Wellensittich, Wellensittiche
5 children, Kind, Kinder
6 woman, women, Frau
7 person
8 mouse, Maus, Mäuse
9 men, Mann, Männer
10 shoe, shoes, Schuhe
11 hutch, Kaninchenstall, Kaninchenställe
12 watches, Uhr, Uhren
13 house, houses, Haus

12 New words
1 swing, over, fence
2 under, bush
3 hole, bush
4 put
5 Poor
6 Quick
7 Get

13 'put' or 'get'?
2 get
3 put
4 put
5 get
6 get

14 What's the word?
1 quick = u
2 give = i
3 smell = e
4 over = o
5 gun = g
6 budgie = b
7 next = n
8 bush = h
9 poor = r
Lösungswort: *neighbour*

15 New words
1 help
2 textbook
3 present
4 real, present
5 help
6 Write

16 Crossword puzzle
1 put
2 write
3 help
4 smell
5 eat
6 run
7 get
Lösungswort: *present*

17 Partners
1 – c)
2 – a)
3 – f)
4 – e)
5 – b)
6 – d)

18 New words
1 shed
2 stupid, zoo
3 stupid
4 best
5 All right
6 catch, back
7 often, visit, zoo
8 cinema
9 tree

19 Some words rhyme
2 live
3 run
4 sure
5 bed
6 close
7 tea
8 write
9 stew

20 How often?
2 The Browns sometimes visit the zoo.
3 Melinda often goes to the cinema.
4 Chris always lets Sandy out in the garden.
5 Softy sometimes eat grass.

21 Crossword puzzle
Across ▸:
1 often
4 wheel
5 grass
7 tea
8 next
10 quick
12 poor
14 eat
15 cinema
16 lunch

Down ▾:
2 farmer
3 best
6 back
9 those
11 catch
13 real

22 Two words
1 *great* / stupid
2 lunch / tea
3 children / rabbits
4 catch / feed
5 behind / under
6 see / smell
7 farmer /neighbour
8 pet / rabbit

23 Odd word out – and out again
2 shoe
3 colour
4 shirt
5 sweater
6 *dress* – shoe – colour – shirt – sweater

24 Pairs of words
2 cage 3 our 4 women 5 bush
6 those 7 write 8 wheel

Unit 4

1 New words
A
1 like, yoghurt, orange juice, coffee
2 like, biscuits, tea, milk
3 pounds, pence

B
1 would you like
2 menu
3 like, start, plate, salad
4 like, sausages, chips
5 like, finish, doughnut

C
1 would you like
2 buy, hamburgers
3 hungry, pizza
4 water, take, ice-cream

2 Similar words
2 coffee
3 milk
4 salad
5 tea
6 water

3 New words
1 meal, breakfast
2 All
3 party
4 toast
5 cheese
6 cake, chocolate
7 drink
8 drink, cola
9 food, drink, cola, all

4 Network
z.B. *chocolate, cheese, doughnut, cake, sausage, salad …*

5 New words
1 need
2 shop, at the moment
3 some, dance
4 Come on
5 raining
6 draw
7 some
8 make
9 need, sugar
10 need

6 The right verb
2 making
3 raining
4 starting
5 working
6 talking

7 New words
1 hold
2 Why
3 only, walkman
4 money
5 wear, T-shirt
6 something
7 other
8 bring

8 Crossword puzzle
1 Why
2 take
3 hold
4 drink
5 money
6 wear
7 finish
Lösungswort: *walkman*

9 Jumbled words
1 bring 2 something 3 other 4 just

10 New words
1 Oh, dear
2 large, size
3 medium, size

11 Numbers and letters
1 hungry, large
2 *breakfast*, cornflakes
3 yoghurt, drink, milk
4 chocolate
5 plate, biscuits
The secret sentence: *Please come to my birthday party on Saturday.*

12 New words
1 holidays
2 Easter, Christmas
3 month, summer
4 term, July
5 When
6 date
7 also, half-term, October, February, June

13 Dates and numbers
2 22.9.
3 29.2.
4 14.7.
5 30.10.
6 1.1.
7 10.6.
8 12.11.
9 8.5.
10 25.12.
11 3.3.
12 20.8.

14 From A to Z
2 December
3 finish
4 large
5 evening
6 31st May

15 New words
1 idea
2 forget, crisps
3 video cassettes
4 brown, jacket
5 Love

16 Pronunciation
[ʌ]: *come*, love, money, month, mother, other, some
[əʊ]: *close*, home, old, open, over, own, photo, poster

17 What are they wearing?
Mary: gelber Pullover, rotes Kleid, blaue Jacke, braune Schuhe
John: weißes Hemd, blaue Schuluniform, schwarze Schuhe

18 Two words
1 often / sometimes
2 at the moment / now
3 at the weekend / on Saturday
4 at lunch-time / in the evening

19 How much?
2 £6.19
3 £12.45
4 £1.98
5 eighty-seven pounds eighty-nine (pence)
6 five pounds fifty-four (pence)
7 four pounds thirty (pence)
8 two pounds seventy-five (pence)

20 Odd word out and somewhere else
2 Wrong word: cake. Right word: week.
3 Wrong word: sweater. Right word: chips.
4 Wrong word: chips. Right word: yoghurt.
5 Wrong word: week. Right word: cola.
6 Wrong word: cola. Right word: sweater.

21 Jumbled sentences
1 Would you like some cake and orange juice?
2 This T-shirt is great, but I need a medium size.
3 Can I have a hamburger and a plate of chips, too, mum?
4 Don't forget to bring two bags of crisps from the supermarket.
5 My mother is making a cake and I'm doing my homework at the moment.
6 My favourite day of the year is June 24th. It's my birthday.

Unit 5

1 New words
1 spare time 2 After 3 jump
4 in-line skates 5 skate 6 fast

2 Making new words
z.B. *are, eat, it, its, me, past, pet, same, sir, star, start, tea, team, tree …*

3 Puzzle
1 spare time
2 jumping
3 fast
4 after
5 in-line skates
6 skate
Lösungswort: *sausages*

4 New words
1 tell, magazine
2 ususally
3 judo, partner, kids
4 chess club
5 use, take photos

5 What do they do in their spare time?
2 pop magazines
3 friends
4 television
5 judo lessons
6 photos
7 in-line skates
8 piano

6 The right word
1 asks
2 tell
3 says
4 talks

7 New words
1 slow
2 leaves, floor
3 shelves
4 tidy
5 complete, sentence
6 complete

8 Say it in English
1 Dad, can I play in the garden?
2 I tidy my room every day.
3 Don't leave your game on the floor.
4 Let's go to the cinema.
5 I'm doing my homework at the moment.
6 Have you got a camera?

9 New words
1 favourite activity
2 hate, hockey
3 never, drama
4 Before
5 add
6 favourite activity

10 The right word
1 after
2 before
3 in front of
4 behind
5 past
6 to

11 Opposites
2 Tony often gives the wrong answer.
3 Tony usually does his homework after tea.
4 Tony hates dogs.
5 Tony likes slow activities.
6 Tony never watches television in the evening.

12 New words
1 policeman
2 public
3 skate park
4 dangerous
5 again, together, path
6 trying, careful
7 legs
8 too, far
9 Look out
10 Too
11 falling
12 Ow
13 foot
14 falling
15 Ow
16 arm

13 One letter
1 *careful*, dialogue, public, budgie/mouse/Rusty
2 foot, dangerous, together, dog/mouse
3 activitiy, hockey, try, Rusty
4 before, feet, leg, budgie/mouse/hamster
5 again, policeman, tidy, budgie/rabbit
6 add, fall, path, cat/hamster/rabbit

14 What do you say?
1 – c)
2 – e)
3 – d)
4 – a)
5 – f)
6 – b)

15 New words
1 grandad
2 really
3 quiz show
4 hour
5 only, cost, much

16 Facts
2 weeks, year
3 hours, day
4 months, year
5 days, months
6 minutes, hour

17 Lost words
1 really
2 favourite
3 right
4 much
5 only
6 much
7 cost
8 only
9 buy

18 New words
1 moving
2 big, boxes
3 waiting
4 race
5 big, car park
6 belongs to, library
7 rough
8 car park
9 Correct

19 Pronunciation
1 wait 2 race 3 skate
4 move 5 too 6 use
7 rough 8 much 9 club

20 Network
Verschiedene Antworten möglich.

21 New words
1 check
2 opposite
3 repeat
4 suggestion
5 space
6 check, each
7 sound

22 Word web
2 smell 3 swap 4 skate 5 sound
6 space 7 summer 8 swing 9 stew
10 sister 11 slow 12 small

23 Make the words
2 dialogue
3 dangerous
4 magazine
5 opposite
6 policeman
7 suggestion
8 usually

24 New words
1 list, snack
2 phone
3 bottle
4 packet

25 The wrong word
2 move
3 lists
4 sound
5 far
6 activity
7 wrong
Lösungswort: *correct*

26 What can you see?
1 a packet of biscuits
2 a bag of crisps
3 a bottle of cola
4 a packet of cornflakes

27 Odd word out – and out again
1 year
2 hour
3 day
4 dangerous
5 month
6 year – hour – day – dangerous – month

28 Pairs of words
2 child
3 near
4 library
5 days
6 feet
7 words
8 in-line skates

29 The right question
1 Who is your grandad?
2 What's in the box?
3 Where's the rabbit's hutch?
4 When can we play chess?

30 Spot the mistakes
1 *haven't* > *hasn't*, she > he
2 skate > skates, pubblic > public
3 its > it's, likes > like
4 to > too, say > says

31 Jumbled sentences
1 Can you go to the cinema with me, please?
2 I'm playing a computer game at the moment.
3 But we usually go to the cinema on Friday afternoons.
4 Let's watch a film on television later, OK?

Unit 6

1 New words
1 Excuse me, places, town
2 looking for
3 swimming pool
4 straight ahead
5 Turn, right, post office
6 swimming pool, left
7 shopping centre
8 hospital, turn, left
9 bookshop, pet shop, right
10 shopping centre
11 café
12 café, bus station

2 Puzzle 'Places in town'
1 bookshop
2 post office
3 bus station
4 park
5 shopping centre
6 pet shop
7 café
8 library
The mystery word: *hospital*

3 New words
1 post, letter, playground
2 stamp
3 back
4 must
5 must
6 throws, basket

4 Jumbled sentences
1 Don't throw my bag on the floor, please.
2 Softy's rabbit hutch is at the back of the house.
3 I must buy a stamp and post the letter.
4 Let's go to the playground and try the new swing.

5 Words with 'st'
1 (z.B.) *start*, stupid, stamp, stand, star, station, stereo, stew, straight ahead
2 (z.B.) *poster*, Easter, fantastic, listen, mister, postman, question, sister, suggestion
3 (z.B.) *best*, breakfast, cost, fast, first, just, list, most, must, past, post, toast

6 New words
1 remember, riding accident
2 was
3 When, was, was, tired
4 wheelchair
5 hard, push, hands
6 easy
7 hurts
8 life, subject
9 ball, ball, most of the

7 Where does it hurt?
1 hands 2 feet 3 arm
4 back 5 leg

8 New words
1 Whose, orange
2 orange
3 banana
4 TV
5 is acting
6 How much

9 So many questions!
1 Where
2 When
3 What
4 Why
5 Who
6 How
7 Whose

10 Opposites
1 remember 2 catch 3 hard
4 left 5 far 6 after

11 New words
1 terrible
2 don't shout
3 you mean
4 mean, idiot
5 angry
6 different

12 Adjectives
2 angry
3 careful
4 far
5 dangerous
6 different
7 hard
8 easy
9 tired
Extra adjective: *fantastic*

13 A word snake
canal, letter, right, tired, draw, whose, easy, yellow, was, stamp, *push*, *hard*, different, throw, wheelchair

14 The right place
1 – c)
2 – e)
3 – f)
4 – b)
5 – a)
6 – d)

15 Pronunciation
1 *bush*, push, put, sugar
2 *hurt*, turn, Thursday
3 *bus*, hungry, hurry, hutch, just, much, mum, must, run

16 Odd word out
1 left
2 whose
3 turn
4 act
5 remember
6 canal

17 Two words
1 *hold* / push
2 is / was
3 mean / remember
4 Catch / Throw
5 most / some
6 Life / Sport

Unit 7

1 New words
1 seaside
2 seaside
3 arcade games
4 beach
5 travel, train, expensive

2 Missing words
1 seaside
2 beach
3 take, pictures
4 buy, chips
5 arcade, expensive
6 swim, water

3 Red, blue, yellow, green
1 train, bus
2 ice-cream, chips
3 seaside, beach
4 basketball, arcade games

4 New words
1 hotel, camp site
2 hot, camp site
3 caravan
4 planes
5 relatives
6 imagine, journey
7 wonderful
8 enjoy, train journeys
9 weather
10 like, cold, hot
11 boat
12 camp site
13 postcard

5 Crossword puzzle
1 boat
2 hot
3 journey
4 caravan
5 enjoy
6 plane
7 postcard
8 wonderful
9 relative
10 hotel
The mystery word: *Bournemouth*

6 New words
1 flight
2 Stay, nights
3 free
4 information

7 The wrong word
2 an arcade
3 easy
4 evenings
5 hard
6 plane
7 imagine

8 Missing letters
2 boat
3 beach
4 caravan
5 enjoy
6 expensive
7 imagine
8 journey
9 relative
10 seaside
11 weather
12 wonderful

9 New words
1 north
2 map
3 signs
4 Welsh
5 difficult
6 alphabet
7 difficult
8 taxi
9 later
10 case
11 hear, woof
12 At last

10 Some words rhyme
2 ✗
3 ✗
4 ✗
5 ✗
6 ✓
7 ✓
8 ✓
9 ✓

11 Partner words
2 – d)
3 – a)
4 – h)
5 – g)
6 – b)
7 – e)
8 – c)

12 New words
1 so
2 Because, go-karts, rides
3 when
4 many

13 The right word
1 b) all
2 a) many, b) some
3 a) every, b) Most
4 a) many, b) Each

14 What does it mean?
2 – e)
3 – a)
4 – f)
5 – b)
6 – g)
7 – d)

15 New words
1 passport control, airport
2 officers
3 May I, passport, madam
4 madam
5 passport, officer
6 if

16 Where are they?
1 airport
2 supermarket
3 school
4 room

17 New words
1 top, high
2 about, three thousand, metres, high
3 clouds, sky
4 view
5 full
6 seats
7 station, bottom, lake
8 lake
9 lake
10 camp
11 funny
12 borrow
13 Maybe, lake

18 One word too many
2 view
3 from
4 the
5 top
6 is
7 great
The mystery sentence: *The view from the top is great.*

19 The fourth word
2 bottom
3 sky
4 expensive
5 hard
6 postcard
7 hear
8 airport

20 Pronunciation
2 view
3 beach
4 enjoy
5 journey
6 weather
7 flight
8 north
9 Welsh

21 Network
Verschiedene Antworten möglich.

22 Questions and answers
2 Why can't you read the sign?
3 Why don't you take the train?
4 Why don't you enjoy the journey?
5 Why can't you borrow Mel's ruler?

Extra

1 Crossword puzzle 'Food'
Across ▸ :
1 biscuit
5 sugar
6 yoghurt
11 doughnut
13 sausage
14 cheese

Down ▾ :
2 chocolate
3 hamburger
4 orange
5 stew
7 banana
8 toast
10 pizza
12 cake

2 Word friends
1 *here*, to the board
2 up at 7, home
3 for the cat, at the picture
4 a cake, tea

3 My profile
Verschiedene Antworten.

Unit 0

1 New words
1 My name is
2 Hello
3 What's, name
4 I'm
5 from
6 German
7 And you
8 live
9 English
10 How are you
11 I'm fine, thanks
12 your
13 Goodbye
14 Bye

2 Word search
yes, name, go, fine, live, what, your, thanks, and, see

3 Jumbled sentences
2 Hi. My name is Lily.
3 I'm Harry. I live in London.
4 I'm Mark. What's your name?
5 I'm Sophie. I'm from Garmisch.
6 Hello, Luke. How are you?
7 I'm fine, thank you. And you?

4 Crossword puzzle
1 German 2 go 3 from
4 and 5 bye 6 my 7 see
Lösungswort: *Goodbye*

5 One word too many
2 I'm 3 are 4 no
5 fine 6 is 7 My

6 New words
1 colours
2 classroom, teacher
3 The board, white
4 What colour is, door
5 It's, green
6 desk, yellow, chair, blue
7 red
8 An apple
9 bag
10 pen, black, pencil, exercise book, book
11 ruler
12 umbrella
13 sweater, shirt, dress
14 to, window, it's time to go

7 The right colour
Tür: gelb; Tafel: weiß; Schreibtisch: grün;
Stuhl: rot; Tasche: blau; Buch: schwarz;
Hemd: rot; Pullover: blau;
Kleid: gelb und grün; Apfel: grün

8 Word partners
2 white
3 chair
4 pencil
5 sweater
6 board

9 The right word
2 What 3 door 4 is
5 your 6 in 7 an 8 to

10 The missing letter
1 apple
2 yellow
3 desk
4 time
5 ruler
6 board
Lösungswort: *poster*

11 New words
1 Have you got
2 I've got, cat
3 that
4 new
5 guitar
6 this
7 bus

12 My book or your book?
Linke Sprechblase: This is
Rechte Sprechblase: That's

13 Jumbled sentences
1 Have you got a red umbrella?
2 What colour is your new guitar?
3 I've got a new poster and a new bag.

14 What have you got?
Von links nach rechts: schwarze Katze, rote Gitarre, grüner Regenschirm, Pullover

15 New words
1 birthday 2 eleven, now 3 old
4 too 5 today 6 happy 7 be, here

16 Opposites
2 close 3 Mr 4 please
5 down 6 come

17 Classroom sentences
2 Can you come to the board?
3 Can you close your book?
4 Can you open your book?
5 Sit down.
6 Stand up.

18 Word search
Across ▸:
sit, open, be, close, stand, see

Down ▾:
go, come, live

19 New words
1 house
2 brother
3 little, sister
4 I haven't got a
5 or, bears
6 How many
7 Where
8 find
9 word
10 spell

20 What's my name?
Captain Jack Sparrow

21 Odd word out
2 desk
3 number
4 or
5 old
6 white
7 poster
8 an
9 song
10 find

22 Questions and answers
2 How
3 What
4 what's
5 How
6 How many
7 Have you got
8 Where
9 Are

23 Picture puzzle
1 guitar
2 number
3 bag
4 sweater
5 house
6 pencil
7 grizzly bear
8 chair
Lösungswort: *umbrella*

24 The missing word
1 spell 2 live 3 find
4 Stand 5 be 6 See
7 Sit 8 go 9 Come

25 The right word
1 I'm
2 you
3 It's
4 your
5 you
6 It's
7 I've, It's
8 your
9 it

Unit 1

1 New words
1 There is, picture
2 family
3 girl
4 There are, dogs
5 picture, friend
6 boy, girl
7 He

2 Crossword puzzle
2 friend 3 girl 4 picture 5 he
6 dog 6 cat 7 family

3 Jumbled sentences
2 There are two dogs in the picture, too.
3 There are four boys/girls and four girls/boys in the house.
4 There's a boy in the picture. He's my friend.
5 There are three families in the house.

4 New words
1 for
2 Mum, Dad, their, aunties, uncles
3 They
4 at
5 His, girlfriend, class
6 boyfriend, pupil, school
7 class tutor
8 has got
9 uniform
10 end

5 People
1 auntie, girl, girlfriend, Mrs, mum, sister
2 boy, boyfriend, brother, dad, Mr, uncle
3 friend, German, pupil, teacher, tutor

6 Missing words
1 has 2 His 3 is 4 are
5 They 6 their

7 New words
1 very, good
2 great, photo of, page
3 we
4 introduction
5 But, exercises, awful
6 late
7 minutes
8 She, American
9 nice
10 favourite
11 situation
12 with
13 I'm sorry

8 'sie/Sie'
1 you
2 She
3 It
4 They

9 Colour the words
Blau: pupil, tutor, uncle, star
Rot: picture, desk, uniform, bag
Grün: sit, see, spell, open
Gelb: old, awful, fine, new

10 Missing words
1 with 2 from 3 in 4 at
5 of 6 for 7 to

11 Crossword puzzle
find, great, sorry, photo, good, awful, nice, late, his, of, end

12 One word too many
1 for 2 with 3 of

13 New words
1 lessons
2 first, lesson, maths
3 French
4 sure
5 room
6 there
7 group
8 week, music
9 first, year

14 Jumbled partner words
1 twelve – eighteen
2 French – German
3 house – room
4 Wednesday – Thursday
5 school – lesson
6 week – year

15 Questions and answers
2 – f)
3 – a)
4 – b)
5 – g)
6 – d)
7 – c)

16 New words
1 You're lucky
2 right
3 silly
4 sometimes, her
5 favourite person
6 ready

17 Some words rhyme
2 chair
3 friend
4 sir
5 great
6 she
7 new
8 right

18 The right word
1 silly
2 lucky
3 ready
4 right
5 Her

19 Word search
Across ▸:
spell, situation, sometimes, shirt, silly, sure, see, school

Down ▾:
sir, sit, she, song

20 New words
1 at the weekend
2 on Saturday, at, past
3 football
4 at, half past two
5 quarter
6 at, o'clock
7 day

21 The right word
1 from, to 2 at 3 on 4 At

22 The right time
Monday: 2.30 – 3.15: guitar lesson
Tuesday: 4.35: bus to London
Wednesday: 6.15 – 7.40: new film
Thursday: 4.15 Paolo
Friday: 4.45 – 7.30
Freier Tag: Sunday

23 New words

1 leave
2 on time
3 hurry
4 television
5 like
6 the same, every, morning, afternoon, evening
7 bed
8 read
9 Then
10 out of

A

1 home
2 get up
3 do homework
4 watch TV
5 play computer games

B

1 away
2 road
3 way
4 drive
5 car
6 mile
7 near

24 Picture puzzle

ball, bag, bed, bus, chair, car, desk

25 English–German crossword

Across ▸:

6 lesen
7 Arbeit
10 aufstehen
12 pünktlich

Down ▾:

1 Meile
2 spielen
3 verlassen
4 fort
5 Auto
8 dann
9 Weg
11 nah

26 Jumbled sentences and words

1 It's ten minutes to school in the car.
2 The pupils go home at half past three in the afternoon.
3 I sometimes watch television in the evening.
4 At the weekend I go out with my girlfriend.

27 New words

1 speak
2 Well, learn
3 listen to, sing
4 piano
5 Learn
6 swim
7 Of course, learn
8 Fly

28 Too many verbs

2 speak 3 watches 4 swim 5 fly
6 does 7 listen 8 play

29 Odd word out

1 day
2 like
3 bag
4 be
5 awful
6 sit
7 work
8 play

30 New words

1 on
2 quiet
3 always
4 bathroom
5 kitchen
6 sandwich, table
7 watch
8 think
9 it's my turn
10 Who is

31 Questions

1 Who 2 How 3 What
4 What 5 Where

32 The little words

1 up 2 to 3 down 4 on
5 up 6 out 7 in

33 New words

1 practise
2 age
3 team
4 disco
5 double, timetable

34 Word groups

2 timetable
3 disco
4 team
5 telephone
6 practise

35 Two words
2 house / telephone
3 happy / quiet
4 practise / speak
5 always / sometimes
6 bag / watch

36 Some words rhyme
2 ✘
3 ✘
4 ✔
5 ✔
6 ✘
7 ✘
8 ✔

37 Kevin's day
a)
2 up
3 kitchen
4 Where's
5 home
6 long
7 watches
8 chair

b) Kevin's dog.

38 What is it?
1 piano 2 radio 3 computer
4 car 5 television 6 homework

39 Boxes
2 numbers 3 colours 4 day 5 family
6 lesson 7 house 8 bag

Unit 2

1 New words
1 hall, ground floor
2 small
3 dining-room
4 living-room
5 first floor
6 What about
7 own, bedroom
8 garage, behind
9 garden, in front of
10 flat

2 Puzzle
1 flat
2 hall
3 living-room
4 bedrooms
5 dining-room
6 garden
Lösungswort: *garage*

3 Jumbled sentences
1 Can you see the car in front of the house?
2 Alice has got her own bedroom.
3 There's a small garden behind the house.

4 New words
1 camera
2 round
2 mountain
4 (tennis) racket
5 (tennis) racket
6 wardrobe
7 stereo

5 Funny words
2 wardrobe
3 picture
4 television
5 favourite
6 mountain
7 exercise
8 situation

6 What is it?
1 tennis racket
2 wardrobe
3 camera
4 garage
5 stereo

7 Questions
1 Do 2 Have 3 Do 4 Have

8 New words
1 question
2 answer
3 sport
4 know
5 swap
6 mother, says, quiet
7 does

9 Questions and answers
1 – d)
2 – c)
3 – e)
4 – b)
5 – f)
6 – a)

10 Odd word out
1 answer
2 question
3 racket
4 mother
5 flat
6 small

11 Word search
Across ▸:
know, like, swim, read, learn, watch, think, swap, play, hurry, drive

Down ▾:
say

12 New words
1 park, bike
2 ride, bike
3 run, supermarket
4 father
5 work

13 Synonyms and opposites
a)
2 father
3 great
4 little
5 leave

b)
2 old
3 awful
4 open
5 answer

14 Verbs
1 walk
2 ride a bike
3 drive a car
4 swim
5 fly

15 New words
1 fantastic
2 wrong
3 petrol station
4 job, bank
5 company
6 Er, supports
7 parents, Formula One
8 postman, gets home

16 Work
Blau: postman, teacher, tutor
Rot: school, petrol station, supermarket, company, bank

17 The right word
1 job
2 home
3 a fantastic
4 drive
5 works
6 supports

18 New words
1 basketball
2 them
3 us
4 Look
5 her
6 him, me

19 Pronouns
1 them
2 her
3 it
4 him
5 them
6 me

20 The right word
1 it 2 She 3 us 4 We
5 them 6 you

21 New words
1 bad 2 talk 3 CD 4 fan
5 band 6 ask 7 wall
8 about 9 want 10 hope

22 Crossword puzzle
1 support 2 practise 3 hope 4 ask
5 know 6 want 7 talk

23 Jumbled sentences
1 My parents always talk about football.
2 I hope you like your new school.
3 My little sister always asks the same questions.
4 My friend wants a Rihanna-CD for his birthday.

24 Missing letters
2 behind
3 company
4 father
5 mother
6 mountain
7 question
8 round
9 support
10 swap
11 wardrobe
12 work

25 Questions and answers
1 – e)
2 – a)
3 – b)
4 – f)
5 – c)
6 – d)

21 New words ▸ pp. 40–41

Trage die gesuchten englischen Wörter in die Lücken ein.

1 The opposite [Gegenteil] of 'good': bad

2 A synonym [Wort mit gleicher oder ähnlicher Bedeutung] for 'speak': talk

3 'CD' in English: CD

4 A person who supports a star or stars: bodyguard

5 A music group: boy-band

6 Say a question: Why

7 *Die Seite eines Gebäudes oder eines Zimmers:* part

8 Let's talk about *(über)* tomorrow.

9 What do you *(willst du)* to do now?

10 I hope *(hoffe)* you're fine.

22 Crossword puzzle

Kreuzworträtsel. Trage die englischen Lösungen an der richtigen Stelle ein.

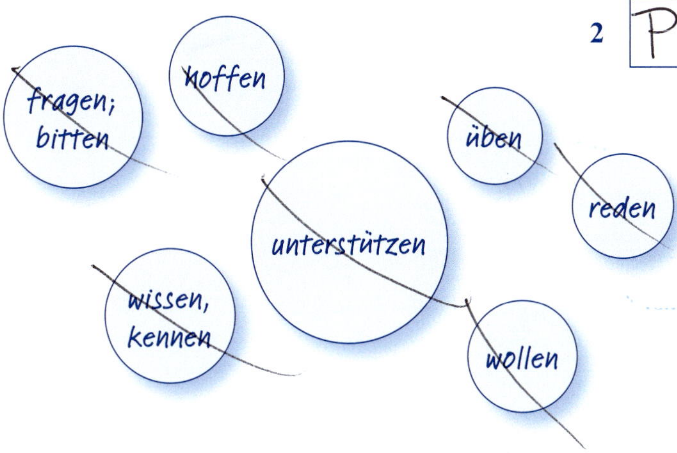

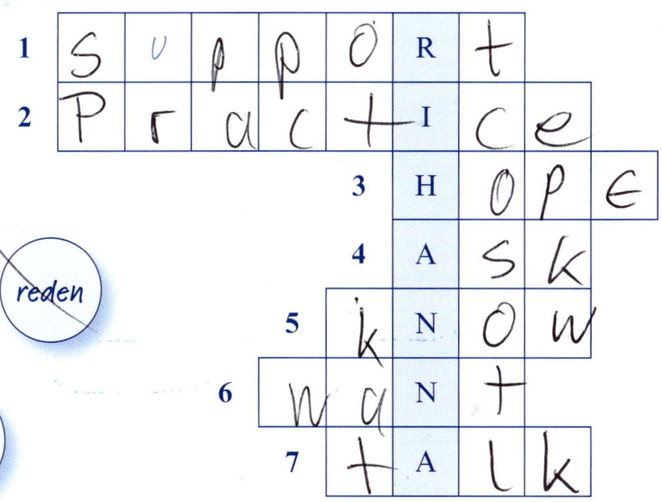

23 Jumbled sentences

Satzsalat. Bringe die Wörter dieser Sätze in die richtige Reihenfolge.
*(**Tipp:** Achte auf die Groß- und Kleinschreibung und die Satzzeichen.)*

1 always parents talk My football. about My parents always talk about football

2 school. I like your hope new you I hope you like your new school

3 asks little always the sister My questions. same

4 a for My his friend wants birthday. Rihanna-CD

24 Missing letters

In den Wörtern fehlen die Buchstaben **a**, **e**, **i**, **o**, **u**, **y**. *Ergänze sie.*

1 _a_ b _o_ _u_ t

2 b __ h __ n d

3 c __ m p __ n __

4 f __ t h __ r

5 m __ t h __ r

6 m __ __ n t __ __ n

7 q __ __ s t __ __ n

8 r __ __ n d

9 s __ p p __ r t

10 s w __ p

11 w __ r d r __ b __

12 w __ r k

Nun überprüfe deine Antwort: Es fehlten 5 × **a**, *5 ×* **e**, *3 ×* **i**, *8 ×* **o**, *4 ×* **u** *und 1 ×* **y**.

25 Questions and answers

Welche Antwort passt zu welcher Frage? Ziehe Linien.

1 Do you know me?
2 Do you want an apple?
3 Do your parents walk to work?
4 Does your father play football?
5 Does your sister like sport?
6 Do we support Arsenal?

a) No, I don't. Thank you.
b) No, they don't.
c) No, she doesn't.
d) Of course we do!
e) Yes, I do. (You're my awful cousin.)
f) Yes, he does.

26 Two words

Ergänze jeden Satz mit zwei passenden Wörtern aus dem Kasten.

bad • ~~bank~~ • behind • fantastic • hall • in front of • living-room • petrol station • round • small • up • wrong

1 My mother has got a job at a _bank_ / ________________.

2 The garden is ________________ / ________________ the house.

3 Where's Dad? – He's in the ________________ / ________________.

4 This apple is very ________________ / ________________.

5 Let's walk ________________ / ________________ the mountain.

6 Your answer is ________________ / ________________.

27 Odd word out

Ein Wort passt nicht. Finde und unterstreiche es.

1 football – mini-golf – racket – tennis
2 bathroom – bedroom – kitchen – question
3 door – plan – window – wall
4 camera – band – music – stereo
5 bank – bed – chair – wardrobe
6 flat – garage – house – park
7 father – mother – parents – answer
8 drive – ride – swap – walk

28 A funny poem

Ein komisches Gedicht, aber es reimt sich. Bringe die Zeilen in die richtige Reihenfolge (1–8).

☐ He's always at home, that's what I like.
☐ He doesn't go out, he sits in the hall.
☐ A good sport for him is mini-golf,
☐ 1 My little brother is very small,
☐ Can you see him? He's there, look!
☐ 8 He's got a German name. It's Rolf.
☐ He's so small, he can't ride a bike,
☐ 3 In the hall he reads a book –

MY LEARNER LOG

Mein Lerntagebuch. Hier notierst du deine Erfahrungen mit dem Wörterlernen.

♥ Meine drei englischen Lieblingswörter aus dieser Unit sind:

____

Wie viele? Ich kenne jetzt die englischen Ausdrücke für …

☐ *(wie viele?)* Zimmer im Haus oder in der Wohnung: ______________________________

____

☐ *(wie viele?)* Möbelstücke: ______________________________

☐ *(wie viele?)* Sportarten: ______________________________

☐ *(wie viele?)* Familienmitglieder: ______________________________

____

1 New words ▸ p. 44

Trage die englischen Begriffe für die deutschen Wörter in Klammern in die Lücken ein.

1 My favourite ______ *(Haustier)* is my cousin's ______________ *(Hamster)*. **2** He's ______________ *(Er heißt)* Snoopy (the hamster, not my cousin!). **3** Snoopy has got a __________ *(Rad)* in his ________ *(Käfig)*. **4** I like my uncle's six ______________ *(Kaninchen)*, too. **5** They live in ______________ *(Kaninchenställen)*. **6** Sometimes they can ______ *(rennen)* _____________ *(herum, umher)* the garden. **7** The ______________ *(Kaninchen)* ______ *(essen)* the __________ *(Gras)* in the garden, but my uncle __________ *(füttert)* them, too. My friend's dog, Sandy, is nice, too. **8** My friend _______ *(lässt)* her ______ *(hinaus)* in the garden every day at _____________________ *(Mittagsstunde)*. In the afternoon they go to the park.

2 The right verb

Welches Verb gehört in die Lücke? Schau dir die Kaninchen an, suche das richtige Verb aus und trage es ein. Vorsicht: Es sind 2 Verben mehr, als du brauchst.

Hi Luke, can you please

1 – let the dog out at lunch-time?

2 – _______ the rabbit's hutch at two o'clock?

3 – _______ to the park with the dog in the afternoon?

4 – _______ the rabbit in the garden at five o'clock and

5 – _______ the hamster, the rabbit and the dog in the evening?

Thanks! Mum

Lerntipp

Bastelt euch ein WORD-MEMORY: 10 Wortpaare (Englisch–Deutsch) oder Wort-Bild-Paare (Englisch–Bild) = 20 Karten; die Rückseite sieht immer gleich aus.

Die Regeln kennt ihr ja: Karten mischen und mit der Rückseite nach oben auslegen, dann abwechselnd versuchen, passende Paare zu finden. Wichtig ist, dass die gewählten Karten immer offen gezeigt und die Wörter laut vorgelesen werden!

Ideen:
- Bastelt immer wieder neue Karten und spielt damit – oder lasst das alte Spiel immer größer werden.
- Bastelt einen Kartensatz mit besonders schwierigen Begriffen.
- Spielt das WORD-MEMORY auch einmal allein, um Vokabeln zu lernen.

3 New words ▸ p. 45

Trage die englischen Begriffe für die deutschen Wörter in Klammern in die Lücken ein.

Jack Hi, Anna. **1** We've got ________ *(Mäuse)* in the garage. Do you know what we can do?

Anna **2** Hm, my aunt is a _____________ *(Bäuerin)*. **3** She has got a ______ *(Schusswaffe)*.

Jack No! **4** I like ________ *(Mäuse)* – but not in the garage.

Anna OK, OK. **5** Paul has got a ___________ *(Maus)* in a cage in his room.

Jack **6** Well, I've got two _______________ *(Wellensittiche)*.

Anna **7** Yes, I know. Oh! I can __________ *(riechen)* my lunch. **8** I think it's ________ *(Eintopf)* today. Sorry – bye, Jack!

4 Funny pets

Komische Haustiere. Welches Vorderteil passt zu welchem Hinterteil?
Setze die Tiere richtig zusammen.

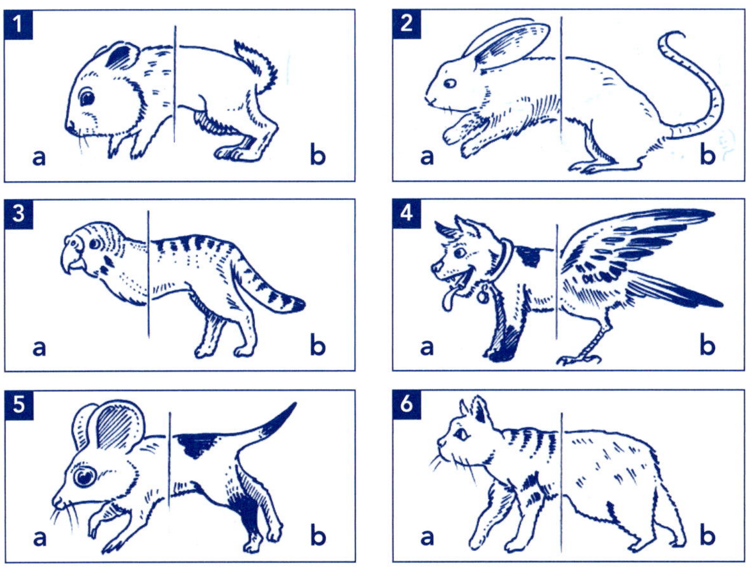

1a + 6b = *hamster*

1b+2a = rabbit

2b+5a = mice

3a+4b = birth

3b+6a = cat

4a+5b = dog

5 Jumbled sentences

Satzsalat. Bringe die Wörter dieser Sätze in die richtige Reihenfolge.

1 friend's ~~My~~ Tiddles. cat called is My cat is called friend's Tiddles

2 in wheel like a cage. Hamsters their Hamsters like their wheel in a cage

3 dog I your feed today? Can Can I feed you doog today

4 the out! Don't mice let Don't let the mice out!

5 good. doesn't The very cage smell budgie's ____________________

6 and like live Rabbits in they grass. hutches ____________________

6 New words ▸ p. 46

Trage die englischen Begriffe für die deutschen Wörter in Klammern in die Lücken ein.

Dear Uncle Bob,

1 Please, please come to ______ *(unserem)* house on Saturday. We can play football in the garden. **2** We've got new ______ *(Nachbarn)*. They're very nice. And we've got a new hamster. **3** You can ______ *(geben)* the new hamster ______ *(seinen)* Namen, OK? **4** You can have ______ *(Abendessen)* with us, too. **5** We can watch one of ______ *(jenen)* great new hamster videos on the internet. **6** And you can see my new ______ *(Schuhe)*. **7** ______ *(Diese)* ______ *(Schuhe)* are fantastic! What do you think? You can't come on Saturday? **8** Well, come on Sunday, ______ *(also)*. See you at the weekend. Janeece

7 Missing letters

In den Wörtern fehlen die Buchstaben **d**, **g**, **h**, **t**. *Ergänze sie.*

1 a r o u n _

2 b u _ _ i e

3 c a _ e

4 e a _

5 f e e _

6 _ u _ c _

7 l u n c _

8 n e i _ _ b o u r

9 p e _

10 r a b b i _

11 s _ o e

12 w _ e e l

8 Right or wrong?

Richtig oder falsch? Entscheide, ob diese Aussagen stimmen (✔) oder nicht stimmen (✘).

1 Pets always smell good. ☒

2 You eat your lunch in the morning. ☐

3 Rabbits sometimes eat grass. ☐

4 Hamsters sometimes run in a wheel. ☐

5 You can have sandwiches for tea. ☐

6 A hutch is a cage for budgies. ☐

9 The right word

Trage die Wörter aus der Klammer in die richtige Lücke ein. Aber Vorsicht!
Lies dir jeden Satz genau durch.

1 (its / it's) Pam has got a new dress. She likes ______ colour. ______ blue.

2 (their / they're) The Brown family have got three children. ______ 5, 7 and 11 years old. ______ names are Rosie, Jack and Kevin.

3 (your / you're) Adam, ______ my favourite friend. Can I have ______ telephone number?

10 New words ▸ p. 47

Trage die englischen Begriffe für die deutschen Wörter in Klammern in die Lücken ein.

Look at the picture. **1** You can see ____________ *(Leute)* at a ________________ *(Bushaltestelle)*. **2** There are two _______ *(Männer)*. **3** One _______ *(Mann)* has got two _______________ *(Kinder)* with him. **4** There are two ____________ *(Frauen)*, too. **5** One ____________ *(Frau)* has got a ________ *(Baby)*. **6** And there's a _________ *(Kind)* with a bag. It's a girl. I think she's on her way to school.

11 Plurals

Fülle die Tabelle mit den fehlenden Wörtern aus.

	English singular	English plural	German singular	German plural
1		babies		
2			Bushaltestelle	
3	cage			
4		budgies		
5	child			
6				Frauen
7		people	Person	Leute
8		mice		
9	man			
10			Schuh	
11		hutches		
12	watch			
13				Häuser

12 New words ▸ p. 48

Trage die englischen Begriffe für die deutschen Wörter in Klammern in die Lücken ein.

1 From the __________ *(Schaukel)* I can see ________ *(über)* the garden ________________ *(Gartenzaun)*. I can see the neighbours' cat, Kitty. **2** Kitty is __________ *(unter)* a ______ *(Busch)*. **3** There's a ________ *(Loch)* near the ________ *(Busch)*. The garden mice live there. **4** The neighbours sometimes ______ *(legen)* an apple there. The mice like apples. But Kitty doesn't like apples. Kitty likes … Oh no! **5** ________ *(Arme)* mice! What can we do? **6** ____________ *(Schnell)*! **7** ______ *(Hole)* Mum!

13 'put' or 'get'?

Welches Wort passt in den Satz, 'put' oder 'get'? Unterstreiche es.

1 Can you *get* / *put* the budgie's cage on the table, please?

2 Can you *get* / *put* your shoes and go out in the garden, please?

3 Can you *get* / *put* that grass in the hole under the bush, please?

4 Can you *get* / *put* the rabbit in its hutch, please?

5 Can you *get* / *put* the dog and feed it, please?

6 Lunch-time! Can you *get* / *put* the stew from the kitchen, please?

14 What's the word?

Finde das Lösungswort. Trage die gesuchten Buchstaben des englischen (!) Wortes an der richtigen Stelle ein.

							u	
7	3	2	5	8	6	4	1	9

1: 2. Buchstabe des Worts für 'schnell'

2: 2. Buchstabe des Worts für 'geben'

3: 3. Buchstabe des Worts für 'riechen'

4: 1. Buchstabe des Worts für 'über'

5: 1. Buchstabe des Worts für 'Schusswaffe'

6: 1. Buchstabe des Worts für 'Wellensittich'

7: 1. Buchstabe des Worts für 'nächste/r/s'

8: 4. Buchstabe des Worts für 'Busch'

9: 4. Buchstabe des Worts für 'arm'

Lerntipp

Wenn du mit einer Vokabelkartei (vgl. *GO AHEAD 5*, S. 154) arbeitest, kannst du auf den einzelnen Karten mit Farbe markieren, um welche Wortart es sich handelt, z. B. blau für Nomen, rot für Verben, grün für Adjektive.

15 New words ▸ pp. 49–53

Trage die englischen Begriffe für die deutschen Wörter in Klammern in die Lücken ein.

Josh **1** Alice, can you ________ *(helfen)* me, please? **2** I can't do exercise 7 in my maths

_________________ *(Schulbuch)*.

Alice OK. **3** It's my _______________ *(Geschenk)* for your birthday next week.

Josh What?? **4** But I want a _______ *(echtes)* _______________ *(Geschenk)*!

Alice OK, then, little brother. Bye!

Josh No! OK, OK. **5** Can you _______ *(helfen)* me with my French homework, too?

6 It's '__________ *(Schreibe)* about your pet', I think.

Alice OK – and no birthday present next year!

16 Crossword puzzle

Kreuzworträtsel. Lies die deutschen Umschreibungen. Dann trage die englischen Verben an der richtigen Stelle ein und finde das Lösungswort.

1	*(etwas an einen Platz tun)*
2	*(Buchstaben „malen")*
3	*(jemanden bei etwas unterstützen)*
4	*(einen Geruch wahrnehmen oder ausströmen)*
5	*(Nahrung zu sich nehmen)*
6	*(Fortbewegungsart, wenn Gehen nicht schnell genug ist)*
7	*(etwas heranbringen)*

17 Partners

Welche Wörter passen am besten zusammen? Ziehe Linien.

1 birthday	**a)** -stop
2 bus	**b)** -time
3 garden	**c)** present
4 hamster	**d)** hutch
5 lunch	**e)** wheel
6 rabbit	**f)** fence

18 New words ▸ pp. 54–58

Trage die englischen Begriffe für die deutschen Wörter in Klammern in die Lücken ein.

Dad Jimmy? **1** Come out of the ________ *(Schuppen, Stall)*, quick! **2** Leave your ____________ *(dummen, blöden)* rabbits and come to the ______ *(Zoo)* with us.

Jimmy **3** My rabbits aren't ____________ *(dumm, blöd)*! They're fantastic. **4** And they're my ________ *(besten)* Freunde.

Dad **5** ______________ *(In Ordnung)*. **6** Can you __________ *(fangen)* them now and put them ________ *(zurück)* in their hutches, please?

Jimmy **7** But we __________ *(häufig)* ________ *(besuchen)* den ______ *(Zoo)*. **8** Can't we go to the ____________ *(Kino)* today? There's a great new film about a family of rabbits …

Dad No, Jimmy. **9** Look, there's Pickle, under the ________ *(Baum)*. Quick, get him. And then we can leave.

19 Some words rhyme

Manche Wörter reimen sich. Suche das richtige Reimwort aus und trage es ein.
Vorsicht: Du brauchst nicht alle Wörter!

1 back – *black*

2 give – ____________

3 gun – ____________

4 poor – ____________

5 shed – ____________

6 those – ____________

7 tree – ____________

8 white – ____________

9 zoo – ____________

20 How often?

Wie oft? Bilde Sätze mit Häufigkeitsangaben: xxx = immer, xx = häufig, x = manchmal.
Achte dabei auf die richtige Form des Verbs.

1 hamster Harry • xx • run • in his wheel: *Hamster Harry often runs in his wheel.*

2 the Browns • x • visit • the zoo: ____________________

3 Melinda • xx • go • to the cinema: ____________________

4 Chris • xxx • let Sandy out • in the garden: ____________________

5 Softy • x • eat • grass: ____________________

21 Crossword puzzle

Kreuzworträtsel. Trage die englischen Bezeichnungen für die Wörter ein.

Across ▸

1 häufig
4 Rad
5 Gras
7 Abendessen
8 nächste/r/s
10 schnell
12 arm
14 essen
15 Kino
16 Mittagessen

Down ▾

2 Bauer/Bäuerin
3 beste/r/s
6 zurück
9 jene
11 fangen
13 echt

22 Two words

Ergänze jeden Satz mit zwei passenden Wörtern aus dem Kasten.
Vorsicht! Im Kasten sind mehr Wörter als du brauchst.

behind • best • catch • children • farmer • feed • ~~great~~ • lunch • neighbour • over • pet • rabbit • rabbits • see • smell • stupid • tea • under

1 Hamsters run in a wheel. They're great / ______________ !

2 We always eat sandwiches for ______________ / ______________ .

3 The ______________ / ______________ are in the garden.

4 Let's ______________ / ______________ the rabbit and put him in his hutch.

5 The rabbit is ______________ / ______________ the bush.

6 Can you ______________ / ______________ the mouse in its cage?

7 The apples are a present from the ______________ / ______________ .

8 Mum, can I have a ______________ / ______________ , please?

23 Odd word out – and out again

Finde die 5 Wörter, die nicht in die Reihen passen, und schreibe sie zu Nr. 6. Sie bilden eine eigene Gruppe. Aber auch hier passt ein Wort nicht in die Reihe. Markiere es.

1 children – women – <u>dress</u> – mice – men

2 cage – hutch – house – shoe – shed

3 colour – birthday – present – party – age

4 cornflakes – apple – stew – sandwich – shirt

5 rabbit – sweater – mouse – budgie – hamster

6 dress – ________ – ________ – ________ – ________

24 Pairs of words

Wortpaare. Was verbindet die Wortpaare? Finde das vierte Wort und trage es ein. Wenn du Hilfe brauchst, kannst du mit einem Spiegel und kopfüber die Lösungen betrachten. Sie sind aber nicht in der richtigen Reihenfolge!

1 child – children mouse – mice

2 rabbit – hutch budgie – ________

3 I – my we – ________

4 man – woman men – ________

5 park – garden tree – ________

6 this – that these – ________

7 get – give read – ________

8 garden – swing hamster cage – ________

push • cage • ~~mice~~ • our • those • wheel • women • write

MY LEARNER LOG

Mein Lerntagebuch. Hier notierst du deine Erfahrungen mit dem Wörterlernen.

♥ Meine drei englischen Lieblingswörter aus dieser Unit sind:

____

Ich spreche sehr gern auf Englisch über ________

____

In einigen Themen bin ich noch nicht so gut. Ich muss noch üben, über ________

________ zu sprechen.

Ich würde jetzt gern noch Wörter lernen, mit denen ich über Folgendes sprechen kann:

das Wetter ☐ Essen und Trinken ☐ Feiertage und Ferien ☐

und/oder: ________

1 New words ▸ p. 60

Trage die englischen Begriffe für die deutschen Wörter in Klammern in die Lücken ein.

A "**1** Good morning. I'd ________ *(Ich möchte gern)* ________ *(Joghurt)*, ________ *(Orangensaft)* and ________ *(Kaffee)*, please. **2** And I'd ________ *(ich möchte gern)* ________ *(Kekse)* and ______ *(Tee)* with ________ *(Milch)* for my sister."

"**3** All right. That's three ________ *(Pfund)* forty ________ *(Pence)*, please."

B "**1** What ________ *(möchten Sie gern)* for lunch, sir?"

"**2** Can I see the ________ *(Speisekarte)*, please? … **3** OK, I'd ________ *(ich möchte gern)* to ________ *(anfangen)* with a ________ *(Teller)* of ________ *(Salat)*. **4** Then I'd ________ *(möchte ich gern)* the ________ *(Würste)* and ________ *(Pommes frites)*. **5** And I'd ________ *(ich möchte gern)* to ________ *(beenden)* my lunch with a ________ *(Krapfen)*, please."

C *Linda* **1** What ________ *(möchtest du gern)* for tea, Kelly?

Kelly **2** Let's go to the supermarket and ______ *(kaufen)* two ________ *(Hamburger)*.

Linda **3** But I'm very ________ *(ich habe viel Hunger)*. I think I'd like a ________ *(Pizza)*.

Kelly **4** OK. Let's get ________ *(Wasser)*, too. **5** Oh, and can we ______ *(nehmen)* some ________ *(Eis)* home with us, please?

Linda All right.

2 Similar words

Ähnliche Wörter. Manchmal unterscheiden sich die deutschen und die englischen Wörter nur durch ein oder zwei Buchstaben.

Schreibe die englischen Begriffe für die deutschen Wörter unten. Dann markiere jeweils die Buchstaben, die sich unterscheiden.

1 Joghurt – yoghurt

2 Kaffee – ________

3 Milch – ________

4 Salat – ________

5 Tee – ________

6 Wasser – ________

3 New words ▸ p. 61

Trage die englischen Begriffe für die deutschen Wörter in Klammern in die Lücken ein.

1 My favourite ________ *(Mahlzeit)* of the week is our family ____________________ *(Frühstück)* on Sunday. It starts late, often around 11 o'clock. **2** _____ *(Alle)* the family sit around our table in the dining-room. Sometimes my cousins are there, too. **3** It's a big __________ *(Party)*! **4** There's cornflakes and __________ *(Toast)*, of course. **5** There's always ____________ *(Käse)*, too. **6** And there's ________ *(Kuchen)* and ___________________ *(Schokolade)*. **7** The children don't __________ *(trinken)* tea. **8** On Sundays they can __________ *(trinken)* _______ *(Cola)*! **9** We eat the __________ *(Essen)* and we __________ *(trinken)* the _______ *(Cola)* and then we _____ *(alle)* go out. It's great!

4 Network

Vokabelnetz. Schreibe alle Vokabeln zum Thema „Mahlzeiten" in das Vokabelnetz, die du kennst. Du kannst auch weitere Strahlen und Blasen ergänzen.

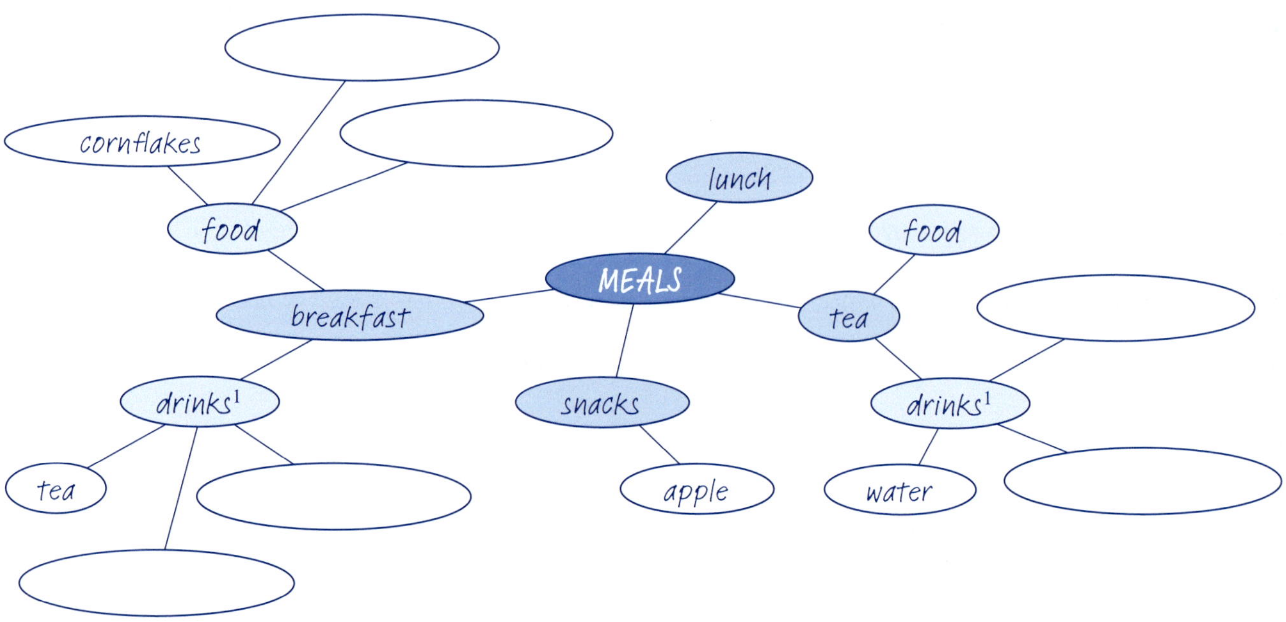

[1] **drinks** [drɪŋks] Getränke

5 New words ▸ pp. 62–63

Trage die englischen Begriffe für die deutschen Wörter in Klammern in die Lücken ein.

Leah **1** I need (*brauche*) a new computer. ✓

Dylan **2** The Market Shop (*Geschäft*) near school has got computers for £129 at the moment (*im Augenblick*).

Leah That's great. But I haven't got £129.

Dylan Hm. **3** Let's go out, play something some (*etwas*) music and sing and dance (*tanzen*) to it. We can ask people to give us some pounds for that. **4** Come on (*Komm schon*)!

Leah What, now? **5** It's rain(ing) (*Es regnet*)! **6** You know, I sometimes paint draw (*zeichne*) pictures. **7** I can ask people to buy some (*einige*). What do you think?

Dylan Well, I don't know … **8** Let's make (*machen*) tea now. **9** Do you need (*Brauchst du*) milk or sugar (*Zucker*)?

Leah No, thanks. I know! I can win £1,000 in the 'Star' game!

Dylan Sure. **10** But you need (*brauchst*) a computer for that …

6 The right verb

Das richtige Verb. Unterstreiche das Wort, das am besten in die Antwort passt.

1 Can you talk to Uncle Mike? – Not now, mum. I'm *eating* / *leaving* / *speaking*.

2 Can you help me with my homework, dad? – Not now. I'm *drawing* / *making* / *taking* a cake.

3 Can you play in the garden with me? – Not now. It's *raining* / *running* / *winning*.

4 Can you draw a picture for me? – Not now. I'm *buying* / *making* / *starting* my homework.

5 Can you drive to London with me, mum? – Not now. I'm *visiting* / *working* / *walking*.

6 Can you buy me a doughnut? – Sh, not now. I'm *dancing* / *drinking* / *talking* to mum.

Lerntipp

Wenn du mit einer Vokabelkartei (vgl. *GO AHEAD 5*, S. 154) lernst, probiere auch einmal, den Wörtern auf den einzelnen Karten Symbole zuzuordnen. Zum Beispiel erhalten dann alle Wörter, die etwas mit „Essen" zu tun haben, als Symbol oben rechts auf der Karte eine Gabel (oder ein anderes Symbol, das dir zu „Essen" einfällt) – ähnlich wie bei einem Quartettspiel.

Du kannst auch ein richtiges Quartettspiel herstellen: Dazu brauchst du mindestens acht Symbole und vier Karten pro Symbol. Vergiss nicht, auf die einzelnen Karten zu schreiben, wie die anderen drei Begriffe lauten, die zu diesem Symbol gehören!

7 New words ▸ pp. 64–67

Trage die englischen Begriffe für die deutschen Wörter in Klammern in die Lücken ein.

Ellen What's that? It's great. **1** Can I ________ *(halten)* it?

Miyu **2** ______ *(Warum)*? **3** It's _______ *(nur)* an old _______________ *(Walkman)*. Do you want to buy it? **4** I need some ___________ *(Geld)*. **5** I want to ________ *(tragen)* a new _____________ *(T-Shirt)* to Lynn's party.

Ellen Yes, OK. My brother likes old things and it's his birthday next week. **6** Now I've got __________________ *(etwas)* for him.

Miyu Great. **7** I've got some __________ *(andere)* old things, too.

Ellen No, no, thanks. **8** Can I __________ *(bringen)* you the money tomorrow?

Miyu Sure. Four pounds?

Ellen All right.

8 Crossword puzzle

Kreuzworträtsel. Trage die Lösungen ein. Wie lautet das Lösungswort?

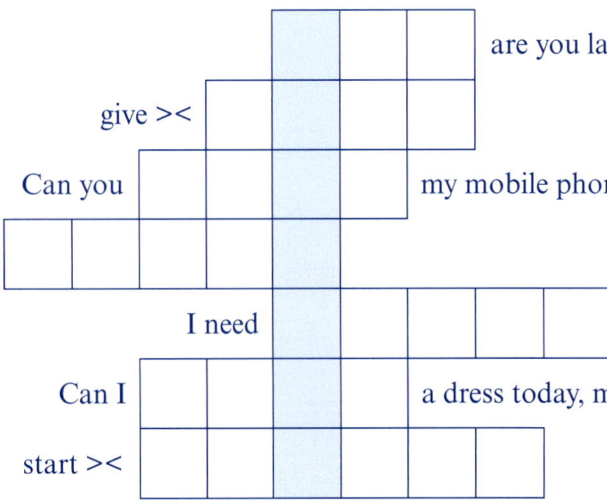

1. ___ are you late, Tom?
2. give >< ___
3. Can you ___ my mobile phone for me, please?
4. eat >< ___
5. I need ___. I want to buy a present for my dad.
6. Can I ___ a dress today, mum?
7. start >< ___

9 Jumbled words

Wortsalat. In jedem Satz sind die Buchstaben eines Wortes durcheinander geraten. Schreibe das Wort richtig neben den Satz.

1 This is a great party. Hey, little brother, can you gnirb me some food? ____________________

2 I'm very hungry. I need themgison to eat, quick! ____________________

3 I don't like the music. Can we listen to some reoth bands? ____________________

4 Bella isn't my girlfriend. She's stju a friend. ____________________

10 New words ▸ p. 68

Trage die englischen Begriffe für die deutschen Wörter in Klammern in die Lücken ein.

1 ______________ *(Ach du meine Güte)*! That's a very small T-shirt. **2** Have you got it in a __________ *(großen)* _______ *(Größe)*? No, not XL – L, please. Thank you. Hm, I'm not sure.

3 I think I need a ______________ *(mittelgroße)* _______ *(Größe)*. Thanks. Yes, that's great!

11 Numbers and letters

Zu jeder Zahl gehört genau ein Buchstabe. Finde zuerst die Lösungswörter und dann den „geheimen Satz".

1 I'm very _ _ _ _ _ _ (5 18 1 22 2 9)! I'd like two _ _ _ _ _ (8 6 2 22 3) hamburgers.

2 You can't eat hamburgers for b r e a k f a s t (10 2 3 6 25 20 6 26 12)!

What about some _ _ _ _ _ _ _ _ _ _ (21 11 2 1 20 8 6 25 3 26)?

3 No, thank you. Let's eat some _ _ _ _ _ _ _ (9 11 22 5 18 2 12) and let's _ _ _ _ _ (14 2 13 1 25) some _ _ _ _ (17 13 8 25).

4 OK. We can have some _ _ _ _ _ _ _ _ _ (21 5 11 21 11 8 6 12 3), too.

5 And a _ _ _ _ _ (15 8 6 12 3) of _ _ _ _ _ _ _ _ (10 13 26 21 18 13 12 26)!

The secret sentence:

_ _ _ _ _ _ (15 8 3 6 26 3) _ _ _ _ (21 11 17 3) _ _ (12 11) _ _ (17 9) _ _ _ _ _ _ _ _ (10 13 2 12 5 14 6 9)

_ _ _ _ _ (15 6 2 12 9) _ _ (11 1) _ _ _ _ _ _ _ _ (26 6 12 18 2 14 6 9).

Lerntipp

Die meisten Menschen merken sich Wörter besser, wenn sie sie im Zusammenhang lernen. Es lohnt sich also, zu einem neuen Wort einen ganzen Satz aufzuschreiben, den du dann mitlernst. Besonders gut klappt das, wenn du dir den Satz selbst ausdenkst. Der Satz kann persönliche Informationen enthalten ('Our Sandy is a large dog.') oder lustig sein ('I'd like a medium size hamster, please.') oder es ist ein Satz, dessen Sinn nur du verstehst – Hauptsache, er hilft dir, das neue Wort zu behalten!

12 New words ▸ p. 69

Trage die englischen Begriffe für die deutschen Wörter in Klammern in die Lücken ein.

Dear uncle Jerry, **1** You know I always go to auntie Janet's house in the _______________ *(Ferien)*. **2** But this year she's working in America from ___________ *(Ostern)* to __________________ *(Weihnachten)*. **3** Do you think I can come to your house for one ___________ *(Monat)* in the _____________ *(Sommer)*? **4** The ________ *(Semester)* finishes on 21st _______ *(Juli)*. **5** ________ *(Wann)* can I come? **6** Just give me a ________ *(Datum)*. **7** Mum says you can _______ *(auch)* come to our house for __________________ *(Schulferien)* in ______________ *(Oktober)*, _______________ *(Februar)* or ________ *(Juni)*. See you, Mark

13 Dates and numbers

Schreibe die folgenden Datumsangaben als Zahlen.

1 Easter Sunday is on April the seventeenth this year. 17.4.
2 Can you come on the twenty-second of September? ________
3 There is no February the twenty-ninth this year. ________
4 Sally's birthday is on the fourteenth of July. ________
5 Half-term finishes on October the thirtieth. ________
6 January the first is New Year's Day. ________
7 Is it the tenth of June today? ________
8 The party is on November the twelfth. ________
9 It's the eighth of May. ________
10 Christmas is on December the twenty-fifth. ________
11 It's March the third. ________
12 Our holiday finishes on the twentieth of August. ________

14 From A to Z

Hier sind die „Anfänge". Finde das passende „Ende" dazu.

1 Monday – Sunday
2 January – ____________________
3 start – ____________________
4 small – ____________________
5 morning – ____________________
6 1st May – ____________________

15 New words ▸ pp. 70–71

Trage die englischen Begriffe für die deutschen Wörter in Klammern in die Lücken ein.

Hi Louisa,

1 Your little party on Saturday is a great ________ *(Idee)*! **2** Don't ________ *(Vergiss nicht)* to buy some ____________ *(Kartoffelchips)* for me. Well, you can buy some for the others, too ;-))

3 Can I bring some DVDs or do we need ______________________________ *(Videocassetten)* at your house? What other things can I bring? **4** And do you think I can wear my yellow dress and the ___________ *(braune)* ____________ *(Jacke)*?

See you on Saturday.

5 ________ *(Herzliche Grüße)*,

Pauline

16 Pronunciation

Aussprache. Ein Buchstabe kann unterschiedlich ausgesprochen werden. Lautschriftzeichen helfen dir. Ordne die Wörter aus dem Kasten (die alle mit „o" geschrieben werden) dem richtigen Lautschriftzeichen zu.

~~close~~ • ~~come~~ • home • love • money • month • mother • old • open • over • own • other • photo • poster • some

[ʌ]: come, ________________________________

[əʊ]: close, ________________________________

17 What are they wearing?

Lies die Beschreibung und male das Bild in den richtigen Farben aus.

Mary is wearing a yellow sweater over a red dress. She's also wearing a blue jacket and brown shoes.

John is wearing a white shirt under his blue school uniform. He's also wearing black shoes.

18 Two words

Ergänze jeden Satz mit zwei passenden Zeit- oder Häufigkeitsangaben aus dem Kasten.

> at lunch-time • at the moment • at the weekend • in the evening • now • often • on Saturday • sometimes

1 I ______ / ______ get up late.

2 I can't help you. I'm doing my homework ______ / ______.

3 I don't see my cousins all week, but we always play football ______ / ______.

4 I always feed the dog ______ / ______.

19 How much?

Wie viel? Schreibe zuerst die Zahlwörter als Ziffern (1–4), dann umgekehrt (5–8).

1 The T-shirt here is five pounds ninety-five pence. £5.95

2 Sausages and chips and one orange juice, that's six pounds nineteen. ______

3 The DVD is twelve pounds forty-five pence. ______

4 They've got hamburgers for one pound ninety-eight here. ______

5 The bike is £87.89. eighty-______

6 Two pizzas are £5.54 in the supermarket. ______

7 Do you want to buy my old walkman? You can have it for £4.30. ______

8 One coffee for £2.75? No, thank you! ______

20 Odd word out and somewhere else

Vertauschte Wörter. Finde in jeder Reihe ein Wort, das nicht zu den anderen passt, und unterstreiche es. Dann schreibe auf, welches Wort aus einer anderen Reihe eigentlich in diese Reihe gehört.

1 biscuit – chocolate – doughnut – yoghurt Right word: cake

2 cake – day – month – year Right word: ______

3 hamburger – pizza – sausages – sweater Right word: ______

4 cheese – chips – ice-cream – milk Right word: ______

5 coffee – tea – water – week Right word: ______

6 dress – jacket – shirt – cola Right word: ______

21 Jumbled sentences

Satzsalat. Bringe die Wörter dieser Sätze in die richtige Reihenfolge.

***Tipp:** Schreibe die Sätze erst einmal auf einem getrennten Blatt auf.*

1 you cake like some Would and orange juice?

____

2 is size. need great, I This a medium T-shirt but

____

3 I a a chips, have and plate too, Can mum? hamburger of

____

4 bags of Don't bring forget to from supermarket. the crisps two

____

5 moment. cake a mother homework at and I'm making is doing My my the

____

6 *(Make two sentences.)* of the day the is My June 24th. favourite year | birthday. my It's

____

MY LEARNER LOG

Mein Lerntagebuch. Hier notierst du deine Erfahrungen mit dem Wörterlernen.

♥ Meine drei englischen Lieblingswörter aus dieser Unit sind:

____

☹ Die englischen Wörter aus der Unit, die ich mir am schlechtesten merken kann, sind:

____

Folgende Übung aus diesem *Wordmaster*-Heft hat mir zu dieser Unit am besten gefallen:

____

Meine eigenen Noten: Ich kann auf Englisch sehr gut (1), gut (2) oder nicht ganz so gut (3) …

zählen: ☐

das Datum angeben: ☐

über Essen und Mahlzeiten sprechen: ☐

1 New words ▸ p. 74

Find the English words for the German words in brackets and fill in the gaps.
(Trage die englischen Begriffe für die deutschen Wörter in Klammern in die Lücken ein.)

Teacher **1** What do you do in your spare time (*Freizeit*), children?

Lisa **2** After (*Nach der*) school? I often go to the park with my friends.

3 We jump (*springen*) over the walls there on our bikes.

Branco **4** We always go out on our inlineskates (*Inlineskates*).

5 We skate (*laufen Rollschuh*) in the park.

Tianna **6** I often ride my bike in the afternoon. I'm very fast (*schnell*)!

2 Making new words

Mache aus dem Grundwort so viele neue Wörter wie möglich, mindestens aber 10.
Du darfst die Buchstaben des Grundwortes mehrfach verwenden, aber keine neuen hinzufügen.

Grundwort: **spare time**

at, term, sit, pair, same, prime, area, set, ~~empty~~

are eat tree

Lerntipp

Aus Exercise 2 lässt sich gut ein Wettbewerb zu zweit oder in der Gruppe machen: Wählt ein englisches Wort aus (möglichst ein längeres), und bildet neue Wörter daraus. Wer nach zwei (oder drei) Minuten die meisten Wörter hat, hat gewonnen. Oder: Wer zuerst 10/15/20 Wörter gefunden hat, hat gewonnen.

3 Puzzle

Complete the sentences and write the marked letters in the right place below.
(Ergänze die Sätze und trage die markierten Buchstaben an der richtigen Stelle unten ein.)

1 My sister plays tennis in her spare time.

2 Look! Rusty is jumping over the fence!

3 Formula One cars are very, very fast.

4 Oh, Rusty. I can't play with you now. I'm hungry. Let's play after the meal, OK?

5 This is my birthday present: new in-line skates. They're fantastic!

6 My little brother can walk, but he can't skate.

Rusty likes | | | | | | g | | s |!

6 5 2 1 3 _ 4

4 New words ▸ p. 75

Find the English words for the German words in brackets and fill in the gaps.
(Trage die englischen Begriffe für die deutschen Wörter in Klammern in die Lücken ein.)

1 Let me ___ *(erzählen)* you about our school ___ *(Zeitschrift)*. **2** There are ___ *(gewöhnlich)* some great photos in it. **3** This month we've got a photo of Nick, our ___ *(Judo)* star, with his ___ *(Partner)* Mike and some other ___ *(Kindern)*. **4** There's a photo of all the pupils in the ___ *(Schachclub)*, too. And some photos of the school, of course. I think they're fantastic! **5** I always ___ *(verwende)* a digital[1] camera when I ___ *(Fotos mache)*.

5 What do they do in their spare time?

Complete the sentences. The jumbled words in the box below can help you.
(Ergänze die Sätze. Die durcheinandergewürfelten Wörter im Kasten können dir helfen.)

1 Siri likes quiet games. She plays ___ every Wednesday afternoon.

2 Ryan often listens to music. He also reads ___.

3 Maya hasn't got brothers or sisters. She sometimes visits ___.

4 Ricardo likes films. He usually watches ___ in the evenings.

5 Alexis is learning a new sport. She goes to ___ every week.

6 Liam works for the school magazine. He always takes ___ with his camera.

7 Ewa likes fast sports. At weekends she goes in the park on her ___

8 Vikram is a music fan. He practises the ___ every day.

djou slosens • drefins • ni-neil staske • opp smeinagaz • poani • seehs • spooth • stivelieno

6 The right word

Only one word really fits in each sentence. Which one? Underline it.
(Nur ein Wort passt jeweils richtig gut in den Satz. Welches? Unterstreiche es.)

Grandad Greg is my mother's old father. He lives with us. He always *asks / says / talks / tells* (1) me, "When are we going home?" And when I *ask / say / talk / tell* (2) him, "We **are** at home, Grandad," he *asks / says / talks / tells* (3), "Thank you, James. You're a very good boy." But my name isn't James. It's Kevin. Grandad sometimes *asks / says / talks / tells* (4) about his work. But he hasn't got a job. He's always at home – with us.

[1] **digital** ['dɪdʒɪtl] Digital-

7 New words ▸ p. 76

Find the English words for the German words in brackets and fill in the gaps.
(Trage die englischen Begriffe für die deutschen Wörter in Klammern in die Lücken ein.)

I think my brother is great! **1** I always help him when he is too ________ *(langsam)*. **2** My brother ________ *(lässt liegen)* things on the ________ *(Fußboden)*? – **3** I put them on the ________ *(Regale)* for him! My brother's room looks awful? – **4** I ________ *(räume … auf)* it for him! **5** My brother can't ________ *(vervollständigen)* a ________ *(Satz)*? – **6** I ________ *(vervollständige)* it for him! (I always know what he wants to say.) What? My brother's age? He's fifteen. Why?

8 Say it in English

What can you say in these situations? (Was würdest du in diesen Situationen auf Englisch sagen?)

1 Du fragst deinen Vater, ob du im Garten spielen kannst.

____

2 Du erzählst deiner Freundin, dass du jeden Tag dein Zimmer aufräumst.

____

3 Du willst nicht, dass deine Schwester ihr Spiel auf dem Fußboden liegen lässt.

____

4 Du schlägst deinem Freund vor, ins Kino zu gehen.

____

5 Du berichtest deiner Freundin am Telefon, dass du im Augenblick deine Hausaufgaben machst.

____

6 Du fragst deinen Freund, ob er eine Kamera hat.

____

Lerntipp

- Wahre Freunde: So nennt man Wörter, die in Englisch und Deutsch gleich sind, z.B. *basketball, computer, hamburger, hamster, verb*. Aber Vorsicht bei der Aussprache!
- Gute Bekannte: Das sind Wörter, die in beiden Sprachen sehr ähnlich sind. Im Zusammenhang kannst du die Bedeutung erraten, z.B. *coffee, December, family, garden, summer*.
- Falsche Freunde: Vorsicht! Die Wörter sehen zwar ähnlich oder gleich aus, bedeuten aber etwas anderes, z.B. *floor* (nicht „Flur" sondern „Fußboden"), *chips* (nicht „Kartoffelchips" sondern „Pommes frites"), *fast* (nicht „fast", sondern „schnell"). Markiere solche Wörter schon beim Abschreiben, z.B. mit einem Warndreieck: ⚠.

9 New words ▸ p.77

Find the English words for the German words in brackets and fill in the gaps.
(Trage die englischen Begriffe für die deutschen Wörter in Klammern in die Lücken ein.)

1 What's my ~~fav for~~ favourite actifity *(Lieblingsbeschäftigung)*? **2** I hate *(hasse)* sport, so[1] it isn't football or hocky *(Hockey)*. **3** I never *(nie)* watch TV or films, so it isn't drama *(Schauspiel)*. **4** Before *(Bevor)* you say 'music': I can't sing or play the guitar or the piano. **5** But let me add *(hinzufügen)*: I like maths, and I like puzzles. **6** So what's my favourite actifity *(Lieblingsbeschäftigung)*? – Yes, it's chess!

10 The right word

Find the right word for each gap in the box and fill it in.
(Welches Wort für „vor", „hinter" oder „nach" aus dem Kasten passt in die Lücke? Trage es ein.)

after • before • behind • in front of • past • to

1 Quick! Lunch is ready. You can go out with the dog ____________ lunch.

2 Always catch the rabbits and put them in their hutch ____________ you go to school.

3 That's our house. Look, there's a little garden ____________ it.

4 We've also got a garden ____________ the house. We sometimes play football there.

5 You're late! It's half ____________ six.

6 We've got ten minutes. It's ten ____________ eleven.

11 Opposites

Gegensätze. Tina und Tony sind ganz unterschiedlich.
Schreibe jeweils den Satz, der für Tony stimmt.

1 Tina likes small bags. >< Tony likes large bags.

2 Tina often gives the right answer. >< Tina often gives the wrong answer

3 Tina usually does her homework before tea. >< Tina usually does her homework after tea

4 Tina loves dogs. >< ____________

5 Tina likes fast activities. >< ____________

6 Tina always watches television in the evening. >< ____________

____

[1] **so** [səʊ] also

12 New words ▸ pp. 78–79

Find the English words for the German words in brackets and fill in the gaps.
(Trage die englischen Begriffe für die deutschen Wörter in Klammern in die Lücken ein.)

1 I'm a __________________ *(Polizist)*. **2** I'm walking around the ____________ *(öffentlichen)* park. **3** Some children think the park is their ____________________ *(Skatinggelände)*. **4** But that's ___________________ *(gefährlich)*. Other people also want to use the park. **5** There they are __________ *(wieder, noch einmal)*, all _________________ *(zusammen)*, skating on the ________ *(Fußweg, Pfad)*! **6** They are _______ ing *(versuchen)* to be ______________ *(vorsichtig, sorgfältig)*, but there's a woman, too. I can't run very fast. **7** My _______ *(Beine)* are tired. **8** It's ______ *(zu)* ______ *(weit)*. **9** _______________ *(Passen Sie auf)*! **10** ______ *(Zu)* late. **11** The woman is ________ ing *(fällt)* **12** ____ *(Aua)*! **13** My ________ *(Fuß)*! **14** Now I'm ________ ing *(falle)*, too. **15** ____ *(Aua)*! **16** My _____ *(Arm)*! Where are the kids? Help me! – Oh, it's only a dream[1].

13 One letter

Ergänze den fehlenden Buchstaben in jeder Wortreihe. Schreibe ein Haustier dazu (Wort oder Name), das diesen Buchstaben auch enthält.

1 c a r e f u l • d i a l o g _ e • p _ b l i c • ____________________

2 f _ _ t • d a n g e r _ u s • t _ g e t h e r • ____________________

3 a c t i v i t _ • h o c k e _ • t r _ • ____________________

4 b e f o r _ • f _ _ t • l _ g • ____________________

5 a g a _ n • p o l _ c e m a n • t _ d y • ____________________

6 _ d d • f _ l l • p _ t h • ____________________

14 What do you say?

Match the people and situations on the left (1–6) with the statements on the right (a–f). Draw lines.
(Ordne den Personen und Situationen links (1–6) die Aussagen rechts (a–f) zu. Ziehe Linien.)

1 You're on skates. You're falling.
2 You're a policeman. You see kids on skates.
3 Your friend is skating on one leg. You think she's good.
4 You're with your friends. You're jumping on skates.
5 Your friend wants to skate on the path.
6 You're skating. You can't stop. A man is on the path.

a) "Look at me!"
b) "Look out!"
c) "Ow!"
d) "That's great!"
e) "Stop! You can't skate here."
f) "Be careful. It's a public path."

[1] **dream** [driːm] Traum

15 New words ▸ pp. 82–83

Find the English words for the German words in brackets and fill in the gaps.
(Trage die englischen Begriffe für die deutschen Wörter in Klammern in die Lücken ein.)

1 My ________________ *(Opa)* Norman isn't very old. **2** He's ___________ *(wirklich)* nice. I like him. **3** We often watch a __________________ *(Quizsendung)* together. **4** It's on TV on Mondays and Fridays for one ________ *(Stunde)*. **5** Sometimes Grandad buys a DVD, but ________ *(nur, bloß)* if[1] it doesn't ________ *(kosten)* too _________ *(viel)*.

16 Facts

Complete the sentences with the right words.
(Fakten. Ergänze die Sätze mit den passenden Wörtern.)

1 There are 7 days in a week.

2 There are 52 _________________ in a _________________.

3 There are 24 _________________ in a _________________.

4 There are 12 _________________ in a _________________.

5 There are 28–31 _________________ in a _________________.

6 There are 60 _________________ in an _________________.

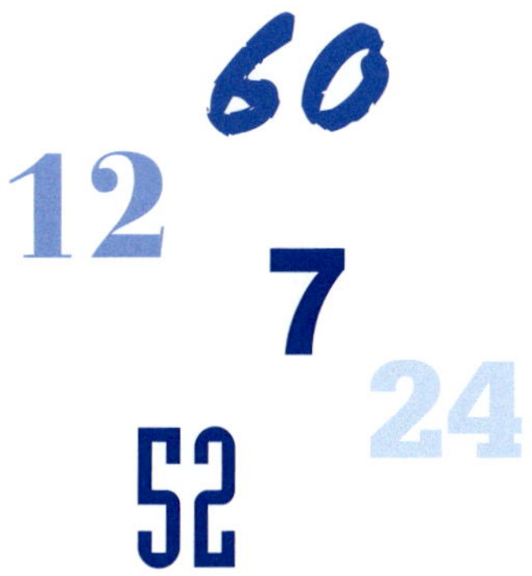

17 Lost words

Some words have gone missing here. Put them in.
(Hier sind einige Wörter verloren gegangen. Setze sie ein.)

I ___________ (1) like this T-shirt. It's red, my ___________________ (2) colour. And it's the __________ (3) size, small. But I haven't got _________ (4) money. I've ________ (5) got 4 pounds. How _________ (6) does it ________ (7)? Oh, it's ________ (8) £3.99! That's great! "Mum, can I ______ (9) this T-shirt, please? I've got enough[2] money."

Lerntipp

Du weißt die Antwort zu einer Aufgabe nicht? Versuche es mit folgenden Tipps:
- Bleib ruhig.
- Schau dir die gesamte Übung an. Worum geht es noch einmal?
- Löse erst einmal die Aufgaben aus der Übung, die dir leicht fallen.
- Arbeite erst einmal mit Bleistift, vor allem, wenn es vorgegebene Antworten gibt (z.B. einen Wortkasten).
- Schau dir die „New Words"-Übung an, die es auf den meisten Seiten gibt. Viele der gesuchten Wörter kommen dort vor.
- Wenn das alles nicht hilft: Mach mal eine kleine Pause. ☺

[1] **if** [ɪf] wenn [2] **enough** [ɪ'nʌf] genug

18 New words ▸ p. 84

Find the English words for the German words in brackets and fill in the gaps.
(Trage die englischen Begriffe für die deutschen Wörter in Klammern in die Lücken ein.)

1 I'm ________ ing *(ziehe um)* to Albert Road today. **2** There are some ______ *(große)* __________ *(Kisten, Kästen, Schachteln)* in front of the house. **3** I'm ________ ing *(warte)* for my friends – and their cars. Here they are! Please be careful with my things. **4** And please don't have a ________ *(Rennen)* to the new flat, OK? … (Later.) Now, where can we put all the cars? **5** Look there's a ______ *(großer)* ______________ *(Parkplatz, Parkhaus)*. Oh, we can't use that. **6** It ____________________ *(gehört)* the ____________ *(Bibliothek, Bücherei)*. Look, can we go over there? **7** No, it's too __________ *(uneben, rau)*. **8** Ah, isn't there a ______________ *(Parkplatz, Parkhaus)* in Victoria Street? **9** ____________ *(Richtig)*! Let's go there.

19 Pronunciation

Match the phonetic symbols and the words.
(Ordne der Lautschrift das richtige Wort zu.)

club • move • much • race • rough • skate • too • use • wait

1 [weɪt] ____________	**4** [mu:v] ____________	**7** [rʌf] ____________
2 [reɪs] ____________	**5** [tu:] ____________	**8** [mʌtʃ] ____________
3 [skeɪt] ____________	**6** [ju:z] ____________	**9** [klʌb] ____________

20 Network

Make a word network for "public places". There are some useful words in the box.
(Fertige ein Wortnetz zu dem Begriff "public places" an. Im Kasten sind einige nützliche Wörter.)

car park, cinema, library, park, school, supermarket, … • books, cars, films, trees, pupils, food, …

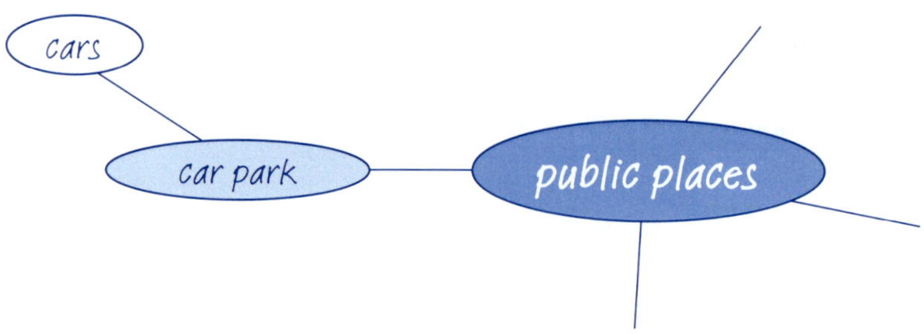

21 New words ▸ p. 85

Find the English words for the German words in brackets and fill in the gaps.
(Trage die englischen Begriffe für die deutschen Wörter in Klammern in die Lücken ein.)

Mum	*Tia*
1 Let's __________ *(überprüfen)* your homework, Tia.	OK.
2 What's the ________________ *(Gegenteil)* of 'big'?	It's 'small'.
3 Can you ____________ *(wiederholen)* that, please?	It's 'small'.
Correct! **4** Can I make a ____________________ *(Vorschlag)*?	Of course.
Let's go to the kitchen. **5** There isn't much __________ *(Platz)* here.	OK.
6 Let's __________ *(überprüfen)* ________ *(jeden)* sentence now.	Mum, I haven't got much time.
OK. **7** Just read all the words with the [s]-__________ *(Laut)* then.	OK. Sister, space, …

22 Word web

Put the English words for the German words below in the web. They all begin with s-.
(Trage die englische Übersetzung dieser Wörter in das Spinnennetz ein. Sie fangen alle mit s- an.)

1 ~~sagen~~
2 riechen
3 tauschen
4 Rollschuh laufen
5 Klang, Laut
6 Lücke, Platz
7 Sommer
8 Schaukel
9 Eintopf
10 Schwester
11 langsam
12 klein

23 Make the words.

Take one piece from each box and make eight words.
(Nimm ein Teil aus jedem Buchstabenkasten und füge acht Wörter zusammen.)

~~act~~ • dia • dan • mag • opp • pol • sugg • usu	al • azi • est • ger • ice • ~~ivi~~ • log • osi	ion • ly • man • ne • ous • te • ~~ty~~ • ue

1 *activity*
2 ______________________
3 ______________________
4 ______________________
5 ______________________
6 ______________________
7 ______________________
8 ______________________

24 New words ▸ pp. 88–89

Find the English words for the German words in brackets and fill in the gaps.
(Trage die englischen Begriffe für die deutschen Wörter in Klammern in die Lücken ein.)

Dad Look, Paul, we won't have time for a big meal today. **1** Here's a ______ *(Liste)* of things that we need for a little __________ *(Imbiss)* later. **2** Can you __________ *(telefonieren, anrufen)* Mum now, please? She can buy the things in the supermarket on her way back from town.

Paul **3** Can I ask her to get me a bag of crisps and a __________ *(Flasche)* of cola, too?

Dad Oh, OK then. **4** Wait, let me write a __________ *(Paket)* of cornflakes on the list, too.

25 The wrong word

Cross out the word that does ***not*** *belong in the sentence. Then write the ▸ letter below.*
(Streiche das Wort durch, das ***nicht*** *in den Satz passt. Dann trage den ▸ Lösungsbuchstaben unten ein.)*

1	Can you	**a)** repeat ▸ S	**b)** complete ▸ L	**c)** ~~tidy~~ ▸ R	**d)** check ▸ A	the sentence, please?
2	Let's	**a)** help ▸ H	**b)** move ▸ E	**c)** phone ▸ R	**d)** tell ▸ N	Mum.
3	I'd like two	**a)** lists ▸ T	**b)** bags ▸ I	**c)** bottles ▸ D	**d)** packets ▸ P	please.
4	Let's have a	**a)** party ▸ Y	**b)** snack ▸ E	**c)** race ▸ V	**d)** sound ▸ R	later.
5	This is a	**a)** rough ▸ U	**b)** far ▸ C	**c)** public ▸ M	**d)** dangerous ▸ F	path.
6	Let's play	**a)** chess ▸ T	**b)** hockey ▸ X	**c)** activity ▸ C	**d)** football ▸ W	on Saturday.
7	I'm really	**a)** careful ▸ K	**b)** slow ▸ S	**c)** fast ▸ G	**d)** wrong ▸ O	on in-line skates.

		R					
5	7	1	4	2	6	3	!

26 What can you see?

What can you see in the picture? Write it under the picture.
(Was kannst du auf dem Bild sehen? Schreibe es unter das Bild.)

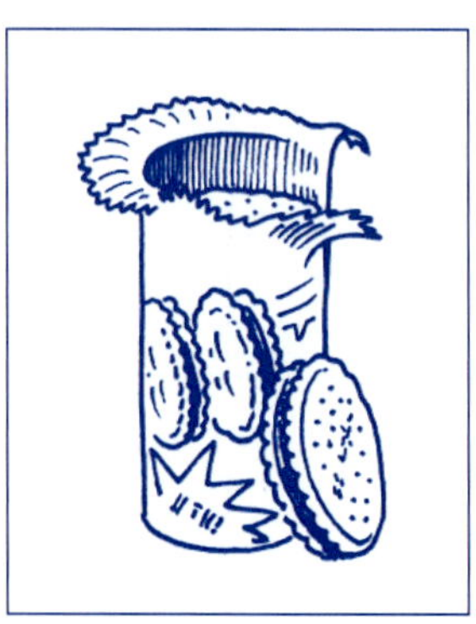

1 a p ______ of
b __________

2 __________
____

3 __________
____

4 __________
____

27 Odd word out – and out again

Finde die 5 Wörter, die nicht in die Reihen passen, und schreibe sie zu Nr. 6. Sie bilden eine eigene Gruppe. Aber auch hier passt ein Wort nicht in die Reihe. Markiere es.

1 partner – kid – year – pupil – grandad

2 shelf – bed – chair – hour – table

3 day – usually – often – never – always

4 sentence – question – answer – dialogue – dangerous

5 postman – month – teacher – farmer – policeman

6 ______ – ______ – ______ – ______ – ______

28 Pairs of words

Wortpaare. Was verbindet die Wortpaare? Finde das vierte Wort und trage es ein. Wenn du Hilfe brauchst, kannst du mit einem Spiegel die Lösungen betrachten. Sie sind aber nicht in der richtigen Reihenfolge!

1 snack – meal path – road

2 right – correct kid – ______

3 big – small far – ______

4 food – supermarket books – ______

5 hour – minutes week – ______

6 woman – women foot – ______

7 house – rooms sentence – ______

8 (to) buy – money (to) skate – ______

child • days • feet • in-line skates • library • near • ~~road~~ • words

29 The right question

Lies die Antwort. Dann stelle die passende Frage dazu. Benutze die Fragewörter what, when, where und who (in anderer Reihenfolge).

1 Question: ______?

Answer: My grandad is the man in the green jacket.

2 Question: ______?

Answer: There are some old books in the box.

3 Question: ______?

Answer: The rabbit's hutch is behind the house.

4 Question: ______?

Answer: We can play chess after school today.

30 Spot the mistakes

Finde die Fehler. In jedem Satz gibt es zwei Fehler. Unterstreiche und korrigiere sie.

1 John haven't got a bike, but she has got in-line skates. hasn't ____ ____

2 He often skate on the paths in the pubblic park. ____ ____

3 John thinks its great, but the policeman doesn't likes it. ____ ____

4 "You can't skate here. It's to dangerous!" he say. ____ ____

31 Jumbled sentences

Bringe die Wörter in die richtige Reihenfolge.

***Tipp:** Schreibe die Sätze zuerst auf einem getrennten Blatt auf.*

1 me, you Can to with cinema the please? go

____

2 – game the a moment. at computer playing I'm

____

3 Friday go we to afternoons. the But cinema on usually

____

4 – OK? a watch film later, on Let's television

____

MY LEARNER LOG

Mein Lerntagebuch. Hier notierst du deine Erfahrungen mit dem Wörterlernen.

♥ Meine drei englischen Lieblingswörter aus dieser Unit sind:

____

Wenn ich über mich selbst sprechen will, kann ich diese neuen Wörter sehr gut gebrauchen:

____

Folgende Übung aus diesem *Wordmaster*-Heft fand ich diesmal ganz besonders schwer:

____

Besonders gern spreche ich mit den Wörtern aus dieser Unit darüber,

was ich in meiner Freizeit gern mache: ☐

wie oft und wann ich bestimmte Dinge mache: ☐

welches Essen ich gern einkaufe: ☐

1 New words ▸ pp. 90–91

Find the English words for the German words in brackets and fill in the gaps.
(Trage die englischen Begriffe für die deutschen Wörter in Klammern in die Lücken ein.)

Ms Black **1** ________________ *(Entschuldigung)*, can you help me to find some ___________ *(Orte, Plätze)* in this ________ *(Stadt)*? I'm new here.

Ms Brown Sure. **2** What are you ______ ing for *(suchen)*?

Ms Black **3** Well, where can I find a ________________________ *(Schwimmbad)*?

Ms Brown **4** Go ________________________ *(geradeaus)*. **5** _______ *(Biegen Sie … ein)* ________ *(rechts)* behind the ___________________ *(Postamt)*.

6 The ________________________ *(Schwimmbad)* is on your ______ *(links)*.

Ms Black OK. **7** Can you tell me the way to the ________________________ *(Einkaufszentrum)*, too?

Ms Brown Yes, I can. **8** Go to the ______________ *(Krankenhaus)* and _______ *(biegen Sie … ein)* ______ *(links)*. **9** You can see a ________________ *(Buchhandlung)* and a ______________ *(Tierhandlung)* on your ________ *(rechts)*.

10 The ______________________________ *(Einkaufszentrum)* is behind those shops.

Ms Black Thank you. Now I'm hungry. **11** Where can I find a nice _______ *(Imbiss, Café)*?

Ms Brown **12** I like the _______ *(Imbiss, Café)* behind the ___________________ *(Busbahnhof)*.

Ms Black Great. Thanks!

2 Puzzle 'Places in town'

Look at the pictures and complete the words (1–8). What's the mystery word?
(Schau die Bilder an und ergänze die Wörter (1–8). Wie lautet das Lösungswort?)

1								p							
2					■						e				
3					■							n			
4									k						
5									■						e
6							■				p				
7								é							
8												y			

3 New words ▸ pp. 92–93

Find the English words for the German words in brackets and fill in the gaps.
(Trage die englischen Begriffe für die deutschen Wörter in Klammern in die Lücken ein.)

Mum **1** Phil, can you ________ *(zur Post bringen)* this ___________ *(Brief)* on your way to the ____________________ *(Spielplatz)*, please? **2** Wait, let me put a ___________ *(Briefmarke)* on it. **3** Oh, and let me write my name on the ________ *(Rückseite)* – the letter is going to Germany.

Phil **4** Quick, Mum, I really _______ *(muss)* go now. **5** I _______ *(muss)* practise before the game.

Mum Practise?

Phil **6** Yes, every girl and boy ________ *(wirft)* the basketball at the ________ *(Korb)*.

4 Jumbled sentences

Put the words in the right order. ***Tip:*** *Write the sentences on a separate piece of paper first.*
(Bringe die Wörter in die richtige Reihenfolge. ***Tipp:*** *Schreibe die Sätze zuerst auf einem getrennten Blatt auf.)*

1 floor, the on my bag ~~Don't~~ please. throw

Don't ____

2 house. back is of hutch Softy's at the the rabbit

____

3 buy a post must stamp the I letter. and

____

4 to go new the the try swing. Let's and playground

____

5 Words with 'st'

Find as many words with 'st' as possible. (Finde so viele Wörter mit ‚st' wie möglich.)

1 **st-** at the start of the word: start, ______________________

____

2 **-st-** in the middle of the word: poster, ______________________

____

3 **-st** at the end of the word best, ______________________

____

6 New words ▸ pp. 94–95

Find the English words for the German words in brackets and fill in the gaps.
(Trage die englischen Begriffe für die deutschen Wörter in Klammern in die Lücken ein.)

1 Do you ____________ *(Erinnerst du dich an)* Ralph's ____________ *(Reitunfall)*? **2** It ______ *(war)* really bad. **3** ________ *(Als)* he ______ *(war)* in hospital, he ______ *(war)* always ________ *(müde)*. **4** And now he's in a ____________ *(Rollstuhl)*. **5** It's ________ *(hart, schwer, schwierig)* for him to ________ *(schieben)* the wheels round with his ________ *(Händen)* all the time. **6** I sometimes help him, but it isn't _______ *(einfach, leicht)*. **7** After some time my back ________ *(schmerzt, tut weh)*! **8** In his old ______ *(Leben)*, Ralph's favourite ____________ *(Schulfach)* was sport. **9** Now I sometimes play ______ *(Ball)* with him: I throw the ______ *(Ball)* and he catches it – ________ of the *(die meiste)* time.

7 Where does it hurt?

Look at the picture and complete each sentence with the right word in the singular or plural.
(Was tut den Kindern weh? Schau dir das Bild an und ergänze jeden Satz mit dem richtigen Wort im Singular oder im Plural.)

1 My ____________ hurt.

2 My ____________ hurt.

3 My ____________ hurts.

4 My ____________ hurts.

5 My ____________ hurts.

Lerntipp

Je mehr Wörter du lernst, desto größer können deine Wortnetze werden. Am besten schreibst du Wortnetze immer auf ein großes Blatt Papier, damit viel Platz für neue Wörter bleibt. Ab und zu holst du dann die angefangenen Wortnetze wieder hervor und ergänzt sie mit den neuen Wörtern.

In Unit 5 (S. 58, Exercise 20) hast du z. B. ein Wortnetz zum Thema „public places" angefertigt. Nun kennst du noch viel mehr Wörter, die zu diesem Thema passen. Erweitere das Wortnetz „public places" mit den neuen Wörtern.

8 New words ▸ pp. 98–99

Find the English words for the German words in brackets and fill in the gaps.
(Trage die englischen Begriffe für die deutschen Wörter in Klammern in die Lücken ein.)

Boy **1** __________ *(Wessen)* __________ *(Orange, Apfelsine)* is that?

Girl **2** That's my __________ *(Orange, Apfelsine)*.

Boy **3** I've got a __________ *(Banane)*. Would you like to swap?

Girl OK.

Boy Great. Would you like to watch a film with me on Saturday?

Girl **4** On ____ (Kurzform für *Fernsehen*)?

Boy No, at the cinema. **5** Ronny Rohan is__________ *(spielt)* in a new film. Most people say it's great.

Girl **6** __________ *(Wie viel)* does the cinema cost?

Boy Oh, £5, I think.

Girl Well, I must ask my mum.

9 So many questions!

Read the dialogue and fill in the right English question words. They are all in the box, but they are in German and in the wrong order. ***Tip:*** *It can help to read the answer to the question first.*
(Lies den Dialog und trage die richtigen englischen Fragewörter ein. Die deutschen Wörter dafür stehen in der falschen Reihenfolge im Kasten. ***Tipp:*** *Es kann helfen, zuerst die Antwort zu lesen.*

wann • warum • was • wer • wessen • wie • wo

1 Let's go out. – OK. __________ can we go?

2 Let's go to the park. – OK. __________ would you like to go?

3 Now! – OK. __________ do you want to do in the park?

4 Let's take our in-line skates. – Really? __________? We can't skate in the park.

5 Yes, we can. Other kids do it. – Hm. __________ are these 'other kids'?

6 My friends. Now come on. – OK. __________ do we get to the park?

7 On our bikes. Oh no, it's raining. You and your stupid ideas!

– Wait a moment. __________ idea was this?!

10 Opposites

Put in the opposite (><) of the word. (Ergänze jeweils das Gegenteil (><) des Wortes.)

1 (to) forget >< (to) r__________ **2** (to) throw >< (to) c__________

3 easy >< h__________ **4** right >< l__________ **5** near >< f__________ **6** before >< a__________

11 New words ▸ pp. 100–101

Find the English words for the German words in brackets and fill in the gaps.
(Trage die englischen Begriffe für die deutschen Wörter in Klammern in die Lücken ein.)

Holly **1** Dad, Justin is really ______________ *(schrecklich)*!

Dad **2** Please don't ______________ *(schreie, rufe nicht)*. **3** What do you ______________ *(meinst du)*?

Holly **4** I ________ *(meine)*, he's a real ________ *(Idiot)*!

Dad OK, OK. **5** I can see you're ________ *(wütend, verärgert)*. But why?

Holly **6** He goes to the cinema with a ______________ *(anderen)* girl every week – but never with me!

12 Adjectives

Complete each sentence with a suitable English adjective. Then make another adjective with the marked letters. (Ergänze jeden Satz mit einem passenden englischen Adjektiv. Dann bilde mit den markierten Buchstaben ein weiteres Adjektiv.)

1 I was in a t e r r i b l e riding accident when I was ten years old.

2 Don't shout at me. Why are you so _ _ _ _ _?

3 OK, you can use my mobile, but you must be _ _ _ _ f _ _.

4 Let's walk to town. It isn't _ _ _.

5 Don't skate on the path. It's _ _ _ _ _ _ _ _ _.

6 My sister has got this T-shirt in three _ _ _ _ _ _ _ _ _ colours – red, blue and green.

7 I can't do this exercise. It's really _ _ _ _.

8 I like this exercise. It's really _ _ _ _.

9 I think I must finish now. I'm very _ _ _ _ _. I must go to bed!

Extra adjective:

13 A word snake

Eine Wortschlange. Die eingetragenen Buchstaben sind immer gleichzeitig Anfang und Ende eines Wortes. Vorsicht: Am Ende geht es um die Kurve und **rückwärts** *zurück! Im Kasten stehen die gesuchten Wörter – auf Deutsch und in falscher Reihenfolge.*

Brief, Briefmarke, gelb, Kanal, leicht, müde, schieben, schwierig, rechts, Rollstuhl, verschieden, war, werfen, wessen, zeichnen

▸

				L					R				T				D			W				E			Y					W

R									W				T								D	R	A	H	S	U	P				S

◂

14 The right place

Where do the speakers want to go? Draw lines from the speech bubbles to the right building. (Wo wollen die Sprecher/innen hingehen? Ziehe Linien von der Sprechblase zum passenden Gebäude.)

1 I need a snack and a coffee.

2 I need some dog food for Rusty.

3 I want to swim.

4 I need a present for my mother.

5 Quick! There was an accident.

6 I must buy a stamp and post this letter.

15 Pronunciation

Match the words in the box (they are all spelled with a 'u') to the correct phonetic symbol. (Ordne die Wörter aus dem Kasten (die alle mit ‚u' geschrieben werden) dem richtigen Lautschriftzeichen zu.)

~~bus~~ • ~~bush~~ • hungry • hurry • ~~hurt~~ • hutch • just • much • mum • must • turn • push • put • run • sugar • Thursday

1 [ʊ] (4 words): bush, __________

2 [ɜː] (3 words): hurt, __________

3 [ʌ] (9 words): bus, __________

____

Lerntipp

Ein Buchstabe kann unterschiedlich ausgesprochen werden. Die Lautschriftzeichen in deinem Buch helfen dir, dich an die richtige Aussprache zu erinnern. Lautschrift wird immer in eckigen Klammern angegeben: [ ]. Eine Übersicht über alle Lautschriftzeichen mit Beispielen findest du in deinem Buch *(GO AHEAD 5)* auf S.120.

Vorschlag: Merke dir die Zeichen, indem du sie nach einem einfachen Beispielwort benennst: [ʃ] ist der *shop*-Laut, [v] ist der *very*-Laut usw.

Die Lautschriftangaben zeigen dir auch, wie ein Wort betont werden muss. Das Betonungszeichen ['] steht immer direkt vor der Silbe, die betont wird: ['veri]. Das kann wichtig sein, denn das Wort *family* wird z. B. nicht wie das deutsche Wort „Familie" auf der zweiten Silbe betont, sondern auf der ersten Silbe: ['fæməlɪ].

Es lohnt sich also, mit der Lautschrift umgehen zu können!

16 Odd word out

Which word does not fit? Underline it. (Welches Wort passt nicht in die Reihe? Unterstreiche es.)

1 stamp | post office | letter | post | left | postman
2 swing | ball | whose | game | basket | playground
3 money | shopping centre | pay | turn | shop | buy
4 hospital | act | accident | wheelchair | hurt | back
5 coffee | remember | snacks | tea | café | cake
6 cage | food | wheel | canal | pet shop | hamster

17 Two words

Complete each sentence with two words from the box. Careful! You don't need all the words. (Ergänze jeden Satz mit zwei Wörtern aus dem Kasten. Vorsicht! Du brauchst nicht alle Wörter.)

act • catch • ~~hold~~ • is • life • mean • most • must • push • remember • shout • some • sport • throw • was

1 Bea, can you help me, please? Can you hold / ____________ the wheelchair for a minute?
2 Hi Andy. Tell me, when ____________ / ____________ your party?
3 Do you ____________ / ____________ Leo's riding accident?
4 Come on, let's practise. ____________ / ____________ the ball!
5 I know ____________ / ____________ good cafés in town.
6 ____________ / ____________ isn't always easy for Jessica.

MY LEARNER LOG

Mein Lerntagebuch. Hier notierst du deine Erfahrungen mit dem Wörterlernen.

♥ Meine drei englischen Lieblingswörter aus dieser Unit sind:

____

Folgende Übung aus dem *Wordmaster*-Heft habe ich diesmal besonders gern gemacht:

____

Ich finde es schwer, diese englischen Laute auszusprechen:

[θ] wie *thanks* ☐, [ð] wie *the* ☐, [r] wie *room* ☐, [dʒ] wie *jeans* ☐ und/oder diesen Laut: [ ].

Ich habe neulich folgendes englisches Wort gesehen/wiedererkannt, als ich …

durch ein Geschäft/Einkaufszentrum ging: ____________

eine Zeitung/Zeitschrift durchblätterte: ____________

Musik hörte: ____________ fernsah: ____________

1 New words ▸ p. 104

Find the English words for the German words in brackets and fill in the gaps.

1 We sometimes go to the German ____________ *(Meeresküste)* on holiday. **2** It's different from the English ____________ *(Meeresküste)*. **3** You can't play ____________ games *(Arkaden-, Spielhallenspiele)* in Germany. That's awful! **4** The ____________ *(Strand)* is different, too. It's really nice, I think. **5** We usually ____________ *(reisen)* to Germany on the ____________ *(Zug)*, but that's very ____________ *(teuer)*.

2 Missing words

*Complete the sentences (1–6). **Tip:** All the words that you need are in here:*

luwateropseasideumbuyba~~different~~elswimdapicturesfrarcadeystakengbeachefexpensivedachipsot

1. People like to do different things at the s____________.
2. Yasemin and Ayse always play ball on the b____________.
3. Simon and Patrick usually t____________ silly p____________.
4. Anita's parents often b____________ ice-cream, but Anita really likes c____________.
5. Some children play a____________ games, but that's e____________.
6. Most of the children like to play or s____________ in the w____________.

3 Red, blue, yellow, green

*Find the right partners Ⓐ and Ⓑ for each bubble **1**–**4**. Then give all three of them the same colour.*

Ⓐ seaside Ⓑ bus Ⓐ train **3** swim Ⓑ beach **4** play **1** travel Ⓑ arcade games Ⓐ basketball Ⓑ chips **2** eat Ⓐ ice-cream

Lerntipp

Denke daran, die Wörter aus den vorigen Units regelmäßig zu wiederholen. Es ist ganz normal, dass du einige Wörter gut behältst, aber andere Wörter auch wieder vergisst – vor allem solche Wörter, die du nicht so oft brauchst. Also schau immer wieder in dein Buch, dein Vokabelheft oder deine Vokabelkartei und überprüfe, ob du die Bedeutung aller Wörter darin immer noch kennst.

Wenn du auf Wörter stößt, die du dir nicht so gut gemerkt hast, bilde neue Sätze damit und schreibe sie auf. Inzwischen steht dir ja viel mehr Vokabular zur Verfügung. Damit kannst du andere, interessantere Sätze bilden, die du dir vielleicht auch besser merken kannst.

4 New words ▸ p. 105

Find the English words for the German words in brackets and fill in the gaps.

Hi Sarah,

I'm at an internet café in Brighton. We're on holiday here. **1** My parents are at a small __________ *(Hotel)* and we kids are on a __________________ *(Campingplatz)*. **2** There's no ______ *(heißes)* water on the __________________ *(Campingplatz)*! But it isn't expensive. **3** The problem was our ________________ *(Wohnwagen)*. It was in an accident and now we can't use it. **4** We can't go to Italy – Tina doesn't like _____________ *(Flugzeuge)*! **5** We can't visit our __________________ *(Verwandten)* in Germany – they're on holiday in Italy!! So now we're here. **6** Can you _______________ *(dir vorstellen)* the _______________ *(Reise)*? **7** It was ____________________ *(wunderbar)*! **8** I really __________ *(habe gern, genieße)* long train_____________________ *(Zugreisen)*. **9** The _______________ *(Wetter)* is also OK. **10** It's _______ *(wie)* home: not too ________ *(kalt)*, not too ______ *(heiß)*. **11** We sometimes go out in a ________ *(Boot, Schiff)*. That's great, too. **12** OK, back to the __________________ *(Campingplatz)* now. **13** Oh yes: No __________________ *(Postkarte)* from me this year! Love, Kyra

5 Crossword puzzle

Fill in the crossword and find the mystery word[1]. It's the name of an English seaside town.

1 It's big and it can move on water:

2 cold ><

3 It's a word for when you travel from one place to a different place:

4 It's like a very small flat on wheels:

5 (to) like >> (to)

6 It's big and it can fly:

M

7 You need a stamp for it, but you can't write much on it:

8 fantastic, great >>

9 It's a word for a person in your family:

10 It's a place with bedrooms and meals for people away from home:

[1] **mystery word** ['mɪstri wɜːd] geheimes Wort, Lösungswort

6 New words ▸ pp. 106–107

Find the English words for the German words in brackets and fill in the gaps.

Fantastic! Only £499!

Fly **AIRGB** now! **1** Take a ___________ *(Flug)* from London to Munich and back. **2** ________ *(Bleiben Sie, Wohnen Sie)* for three _____________ *(Nächte)* in the fantastic **AIRGB** Hotel in Munich. **3** Get a ________ *(kostenloses)* souvenir of Munich.

All for only £499!

4 For more _________________________ *(Informationen)* go to www.airgb…

7 The wrong word

Only two of the three choices[1] in each sentence are right. Cross out the wrong one.

1. Hi Serena, I'm on holiday in Wales. I'm staying *at the seaside* | ~~*in the shopping centre*~~ | *in the mountains.*
2. My parents and my brother are with me. We're staying at *a hotel* | *a camp site* | *an arcade*.
3. The meals here are wonderful! They aren't *expensive* | *free* | *easy*.
4. We're only staying for seven *evenings* | *nights* | *days*. Then we must go home.
5. The weather is good. It's not too *cold* | *hard* | *hot*.
6. We often go on *plane* | *boat* | *train* journeys. They're great.
7. I always *like* | *enjoy* | *imagine* our holidays! Bye now, Lilly.

8 Missing letters

Complete the words with the letters **a**, **e**, **i**, **o**, **u** *or* **y**.
Tip: *The German words are all in the box below.*

1 a r c a d e
2 b _ _ t
3 b _ _ ch
4 c _ r _ v _ n
5 _ n j _ _
6 _ x p _ n s _ v _
7 _ m _ g _ n _
8 j _ _ r n _ _
9 r _ l _ t _ v _
10 s _ _ s _ d _
11 w _ _ t h _ r
12 w _ n d _ r f _ l

genießen Meeresküste Reise Schiff Spielhalle Strand teuer Verwandte/r sich vorstellen Wetter Wohnwagen wunderbar

[1] **choice** [tʃɔɪs] Möglichkeit

9 New words ▸ pp. 108–109

Find the English words for the German words in brackets and fill in the gaps.

Jamie is visiting his cousin David in Wales. They're on their way from the bus station to David's home.

Jamie Are you sure we're on the right road?

David Of course I'm sure. I know my way home!

Jamie **1** But don't you live far away from here, in the __________ *(Norden)*?

David **2** Yes, but I can read a _______ *(Landkarte)*.

Jamie **3** But can you read the __________ *(Schilder, Zeichen)*, too?

4 They're all in __________ *(Walisisch)*.

David Of course I can read them. **5** It's not ________________ *(schwierig)*.

6 They use the same ________________ *(Alphabet)*.

Jamie **7** But 'Gymru' means 'Wales', that **is** ________________ *(schwierig)*!

8 Can't we take a _______ *(Taxi)*?

David Too late.

– **9 Two hours** _________ *(später)* **…**

Jamie I can't go on. **10** This ________ *(Koffer)* is terrible.

David Sh! Listen! **11** Can you ________ *(hören)* the ________ *(Wauwau)*? That's Tinka, my dog.

Jamie **12** ___________ *(Endlich)*!

10 Some words rhyme

Which pairs of words rhyme[1] (✔) and which don't rhyme (✘)?

1 case – race ✔	**4** map – job ☐	**7** site – flight ☐
2 hear – wear ☐	**5** woof – move ☐	**8** stay – they ☐
3 hot – boat ☐	**6** sign – fine ☐	**9** train – plane ☐

11 Partner words

Find the partner word (a–h) for each word (1–8) and draw a line.

3 difficult **h** fly **8** Wales **f** listen **5** case **a** hard **g** bag **7** seaside **1** hear **2** woof **d** dog **e** beach **6** letter **c** Welsh **4** travel **b** postcard

[1] (to) **rhyme** [raɪm] sich reimen

12 New words ▸ p. 112

Find the English words for the German words in brackets and fill in the gaps.

Grace **1** Why is Abby ____ *(so)* angry!

Ricky **2** ______________ *(Weil)* she can't go to that park where the _________________ *(Gokarts)* and the other __________ *(Karusselle)* are.

Grace But she was there yesterday. **3** Is she always angry _________ *(wenn)* she can't do what she wants to do?

Ricky Well, yes. Mum says the park is too expensive. **4** Not _________ *(viele)* parents have got the money for it.

Grace She's right, of course. And your sister must learn that she can't always do what she wants to do.

Ricky Yes, but don't forget: She's only four.

13 The right word

Put the words in brackets in the right gap, (a) or (b).

1 *(all/~~much~~)* Hurry! We haven't got much (a) time.

___________ (b) the kids are waiting for us.

2 *(many/some)* Look! There aren't ___________ (a) pets in this pet shop, only ___________ (b) hamsters.

3 *(every/most)* I know ___________ (a) dog in town. ___________ (b) of them are my friends.

4 *(each/many)* There are so ___________ (a) playgrounds here. ___________ (b) of them is different.

14 What does it mean?

What does the underlined word in each sentence mean? Draw a line to the right German word.

1 I always play arcade games <u>when</u> I'm at the seaside. — **a)** als

2 <u>Excuse me</u>, can you tell me the way to the beach, please? — **b)** Tut mir leid

3 I was always hungry <u>when</u> I was on holiday. — **c)** wenn

4 Look, there's a band playing on the beach. Let's <u>listen to</u> them. — **d)** hören

5 <u>I'm sorry</u>, but I can't go out in the boat with you today. — **e)** Entschuldigung

6 Can you tell me <u>when</u> the programme starts? — **f)** zuhören

7 I think I can <u>hear</u> music – oh, it's your phone. — **g)** wann

15 New words ▸ p. 113

Find the English words for the German words in brackets and fill in the gaps.

I like to go to India and see my relatives there, but I hate the flights. Why? Because there's not much space in a plane. And because the films are usually bad. **1** And because I hate ______________________ *(die Reisepasskontrolle)* at the ______________ *(Flughafen)*. **2** The ______________ *(Beamten)* aren't always very nice. **3** They say silly things like '________ *(Darf ich)* see your ______________ *(Reisepass)*, ____________ *(gnädige Frau)*?' **4** Well, I'm a young girl, not a '____________' *(gnädige Frau)*! **5** And I've got the ______________ *(Reisepass)* in my hand – the ____________ *(Beamte/Beamtin)* can just take it. **6** Then they ask ___ *(ob)* I've got a bottle of water in my bag. Well, no! I'm not stupid. I know you can't take drinks[1] with you on the plane. And … What? – Yes, I know. They're only doing their job.

16 Where are they?

Where are the people? Finish the place words.

1 At the a____________: "May I see your passport, please, madam?" – Mrs Sharma: "Here it is."

2 In the s____________________: "May I help you with your bags, Mrs Link?" – "Oh, yes, please. Thanks, Tim."

3 At s__________: "May I ask a question, please, sir?" – "Yes, what is it, Alicia?"

4 In Emily's r________: "May I watch the film with you and Jack?" – "No! Watch it in your own room."

Lerntipp

Wenn du einmal vergessen hast, wie ein englisches Wort auf Deutsch heißt, kannst du in einem Wörterbuch oder in deinem Englischbuch nachschlagen (*GO AHEAD 5*, S. 172–176). In solchen Wörterverzeichnissen sind die Wörter alphabetisch sortiert.

Um den Umgang mit einer alphabetischen Liste zu üben, eignen sich Spiele: Schreibe z. B. die neuen Wörter aus Unit 7 auf kleine Zettelchen und ordne diese dann alphabetisch. Oder ihr spielt zusammen: Wer zuerst die ersten 10/15/20 Wörter dieser Unit richtig alphabetisch geordnet hat, hat gewonnen.

Wichtig: Wenn es mehrere Wörter gibt, die mit demselben Buchstaben anfangen, kommt es auf den zweiten Buchstaben der Wörter an. Wenn es mehrere Wörter gibt, bei denen die ersten beiden Buchstaben gleich sind, ist der dritte Buchstabe entscheidend – usw.

Schreibe nun diese Wörter in der richtigen alphabetischen Reihefolge auf:

up · under · usually · unit · umbrella · us · uniform · uncle · use

Schau beim Buchstaben **U** im Wörterverzeichnis deines Buches (S. 176) nach, ob du es richtig gemacht hast.

[1] **drinks** [drɪŋks] Getränke

17 New words ▸ pp. 114–116

Find the English words for the German words in brackets and fill in the gaps.

Hi, Connor! Can you hear me? No, I'm not at home. **1** We're in Germany at the moment, on ______ *(Spitze)* of a very ______ *(hohen)* mountain. What? It's called the 'Zugspitze'. **2** It's ______ *(ungefähr)* three ______ *(dreitausend)* ______ *(Meter)* ______ *(hoch)*. We're so lucky. **3** There are no ______ *(Wolken)* in the ______ *(Himmel)*. **4** The ______ *(Ausblick)* is fantastic. Yes, there's a train that goes up the mountain. What? **5** Well, I hope we can go down in the cable car[1] but it's often ______ *(voll)*. **6** No, I don't think there are ______ *(Sitze, Sitzplätze)* in the cable car. **7** The cable car ______ *(Bahnhof, Station)* at the ______ *(Boden, Fuß)* of the mountain is near a ______ *(See)*. You can walk around it. What? **8** No, not around the station, around the ______ *(See)*, of course! **9** No, you can't swim in the ______ *(See)*. It's too cold. **10** No, you can't ______ *(zelten)* there. Connor, it's December! **11** Now stop it, that isn't ______ *(witzig, komisch)*. We're staying at a little hotel. The rooms are small, but the people are very nice. **12** I want to ask them if I can ______ *(mir ausleihen, borgen)* one of their bikes. **13** ______ *(vielleicht)* I can ride the bike around the ______ *(See)* then.

18 One word too many

Find the word that does not belong in the sentence and cross it out.
Then write it on the line below (from 1–7) and get the mystery sentence.

1 Mum, when can we go back ~~the~~ home? I'm tired!

2 Look! Can you see the top view of the mountain?

3 It isn't far to the top from now.

4 The station? Go the straight ahead here, and it's on your right.

5 The mountain is about a thousand metres top high.

6 You can also take the train up the mountain, but it is often is full.

7 I don't like really great high mountains, but I love the seaside.

The mystery sentence:

The ____!

[1] **cable car** ['keɪbl kɑː] Seilbahn

19 The fourth[1] word

*Find the fourth word and fill it in. **Tip:** The words are all in the box below.*

1 place – site enjoy – like
2 night – day top – ________
3 boat – lake plane – ________
4 hot – cold free – ________
5 fantastic – wonderful difficult – ________
6 case – bag letter – ________
7 look – see listen – ________
8 train – station plane – ________

airport • bottom • expensive • hear • hard • like • postcard • sky

20 Pronunciation

Match the phonetic symbols[2] and the words from the box. Careful: You don't need all the words.

beach • cloud • enjoy • flight • journey • lake • north • seat • ~~sign~~ • view • weather • Welsh

1 [saɪn] sign
2 [vjuː] ________
3 [biːtʃ] ________
4 [ɪn'dʒɔɪ] ________
5 ['dʒɜːni] ________
6 ['weðə] ________
7 [flaɪt] ________
8 [nɔːθ] ________
9 [welʃ] ________

21 Network

Make a word network for "holidays". The questions below and the words in the box can help you.

mountain, lake, relatives, seaside … • camp, swim, visit, walk … • boat, car, plane, train … • campsite, caravan, hotel, …

[1] **fourth** [fɔːθ] vierte/r/s [2] **phonetic symbols** [fə'netɪk 'sɪmblz] Lautschrift

22 Questions and answers

First read the answer. Then write the question. Use 'can't' or 'don't' and the words in brackets.

1 (like • planes) Why don't you like planes? – Because there isn't much space.

2 (read • sign) Why ______________________________ ?

Because it's in Welsh.

3 (take • train) Why ______________________________ ?

Because you can't always get a seat.

4 (enjoy • journey) Why ______________________________ ?

Because it's always much too long.

5 (borrow • Mel's ruler) Why ______________________________ ?

Because she's using it at the moment.

MY LEARNER LOG

Mein Lerntagebuch. Hier notierst du deine Erfahrungen mit dem Wörterlernen.

♥ Meine drei englischen Lieblingswörter aus dieser Unit sind:

____

Diese Wörter aus der Unit kann ich besonders gut gebrauchen, um über meine eigenen Ferien zu sprechen:

____

Ich möchte gern noch besser lernen, auf Englisch:

höflich zu sein ☐, witzig zu sein ☐, zu diskutieren ☐, eine Geschichte zu erzählen ☐ und/oder

____

Am Ende dieses *Wordmaster*-Heftes gebe ich mir folgende Englisch-Noten von 1 (= sehr gut) bis 5 (= mangelhaft):

(beim Sprechen) für meine Aussprache: ☐

(beim Lesen oder Hören) für das Wiedererkennen von Wörtern: ☐

(beim Sprechen oder Schreiben) für die Benutzung von Wörtern, die schon vorgekommen sind: ☐

(beim Lesen oder Hören) für das Verstehen von Texten, auch wenn ich nicht alle Wörter kenne: ☐

(beim Schreiben) für die richtige Schreibweise von Wörtern: ☐

1 Crossword puzzle 'Food'

Look at the German words below. What are they in English?
Now find the right place for them in the crossword.

~~Apfel~~ • Banane • Berliner, Krapfen • Eintopf • Hamburger • Joghurt • Käse • Keks • Kuchen • Orange, Apfelsine • Pizza • Schokolade • Toast • Wurst • Zucker

■	■	■	■	1	i		2	u	i		■	■
■	■	■	3	■	■	■		■	■	■	4 o	■
5	u		a		■	6	o			u		
	■	■		■	7	■		■	■	■	a	■
e	■	■		■		■	o	■	■	■		■
	■	■	u	■		■		■	■	■		■
■	8	■		■		■	9 a	p	10 p	l	e	■
11	o	u				u		■	i	■	■	■
■	a	■	e	■		■	e	■		■	■	■
■		■		■	■	12	■	■		■	■	■
■		■	■	■	13	a	u		a		e	■
■	■	■	■	■	■		■	■	■	■	■	■
■	14		e	e		e	■	■	■	■	■	■

2 Word friends

Each verb (1–4) goes with only two of the words/phrases[1] below. Circle the right two.

[1] **phrase** [freɪz] Ausdruck

3 My profile

Complete this "self-portrait" with as many details as possible.
(Mein Profil. Fülle den Steckbrief über dich selbst mit möglichst vielen Einzelheiten aus.)

Name: ______________________________

Age ______________________________

Birthday: ______________________________

School: ______________________________

Favourite school subject(s): ______________________________

Parents: ______________________________

Brothers and sisters: ______________________________

Friends: ______________________________

Girlfriend/Boyfriend: ______________________________

Favourite colour: ______________________________

Favourite band: ______________________________

Favourite pet: ______________________________

Favourite activity/sport: ______________________________

Favourite TV programme: ______________________________

Favourite food/snack: ______________________________

Favourite drink: ______________________________

Favourite holiday (where? what?): ______________________________

Favourite 3 English words: ______________________________

____

Favourite ______________________:

____